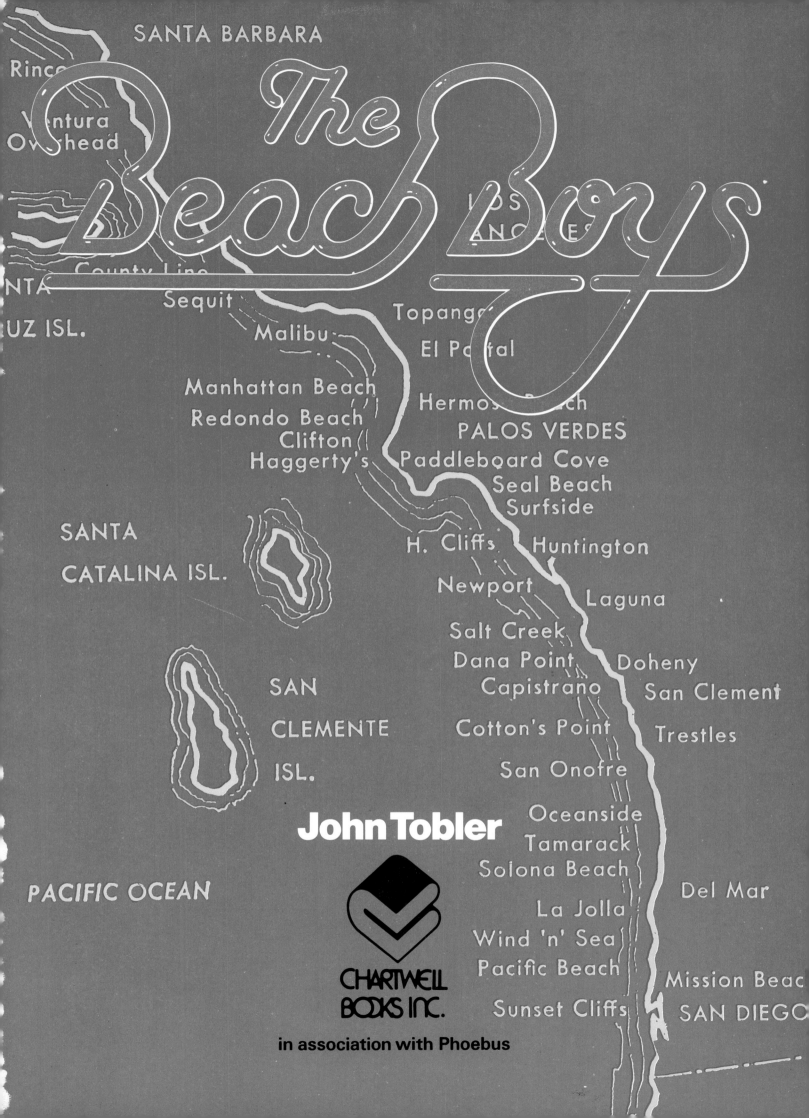

Edited by Jeremy Pascall & Pamela Harvey
Designed by Rob Burt

The publishers gratefully acknowledge the help of Charles Webster & Capitol Records, Dave Walters, Steve Brendell & WEA Records and Raymond McCarthy. Chapter openers: artwork Peter Campbell

Published by Chartwell Books Inc
A division of Book Sales Inc
110 Enterprise Avenue
Secaucus, New Jersey 07094

Library of Congress Catalog Card
Number: 77-73805

ISBN 0-89009-174-9

This edition © 1978 Phoebus
Publishing Company/BPC
Publishing Limited,
169 Wardour Street,
London W1A 2JX

Made and printed in Great Britain by Waterlow
(Dunstable) Limited

Contents

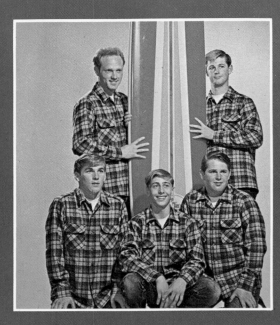

Capitol

Capitol

All Summer Long
1961-65

Rock music at the start of the '60s was at a crossroads. Rock & roll, as typified by Jerry Lee Lewis, Little Richard, Chuck Berry and the rest, was dying, and there didn't seem to be anything significant on the way up to replace it. The new decade was beginning to look suspiciously like the '50s, until two important, but apparently unconnected, events occurred in 1961.

On January 20 of that year came the inauguration of President John Kennedy, a much more vibrant personality than most of his predecessors. At the same time, the relatively ignored state of California suddenly hit the headlines nationally, portrayed as the future of America — although why it had been overlooked before remains a mystery. Kennedy, youthful and attractive, and California, a state with enormous natural beauty and enough variety of climate to satisfy anyone's desires, became the twin symbols of hope for America in the '60s, and apart from anything else, produced a previously undiscovered pride in young Californians.

California Saga

Of course, there had been rock in the Golden State before, but nothing which couldn't equally claim to have been initiated somewhere else. Until, that is, three brothers who lived in Hawthorne, a suburb of Los Angeles, decided to start a group with their cousin and another friend. It wasn't long before that group became the spearhead of a West Coast music scene which, even many years later, remains as one of the most exciting and innovative in popular music.

Brian Wilson was born on June 20, 1942, Dennis Wilson on December 4, 1944, and Carl Wilson on December 21, 1946. Their parents' names were Murry and Audree; Wilson Senior was an amateur songwriter, which came in very useful when the fateful decision to form a group was made. Michael Love, a cousin of the Wilson boys, was born on March 15, 1941. He and Brian became particularly friendly due

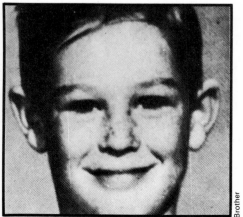

to their mutual interest in the harmony aspects of pop music, with special reference to the songs of the Everly Brothers, and it wasn't long before Brian organized his bothers and Mike

The young Wilson brothers: Brian, 7 (left); Dennis, 10 (below) and Carl, 8 (right).

singing more complicated harmonies like those of the Four Freshmen.

But there always seemed to be one voice missing, and Audree Wilson was usually prevailed upon to make up the numbers, until an accident strangely provided the final piece of the harmony jigsaw. Brian was playing football at Hawthorne High School one day, when he put a team-mate in a difficult position, the result being that Alan Jardine got his leg broken. From this somewhat unlikely start, a friendship developed between Brian and Al (born September 3, 1942), and the group was complete.

Apart from having exactly the right voice to complement the other four, Al was a better musician than all the others except Carl, who was even then an accomplished guitarist. Al in fact played stand up double bass, and was deeply involved in folk music, another asset which was to prove useful in the group getting their first all-important break. Dennis was talked into learning the drums, Brian started seriously to learn piano, and Mike played saxophone for a short while, although he soon reverted to a simple singing role.

The big chance to put all this theorizing into action came in September, 1961, when Murry and Audree Wilson took an extended holiday in Mexico City, leaving the boys with some money to buy food. Instead of food, the money was spent on renting musical instruments, and Carl and the Passions (a name which would reappear more than 11 years later) began to practice playing the music they enjoyed, from the Everly Brothers and Chuck Berry to contemporary hits like *Barbara-Ann* by the Regents.

It wasn't long before they dropped the name of Carl and the Passions, and at about the same time Dennis Wilson,

a very keen surfer, suggested that they write some songs of their own on the subject of his favorite sport. So Mike wrote some words, which Brian put to music, the result having the commendably direct title of *Surfin'*.

This was the point when Murry Wilson's songwriting career and Al Jardine's interest in folk paid off for the group. Murry's publisher, Hite Morgan, asked whether Murry knew of anyone who could make a demo for him of a folk song, and Al was the obvious person to recommend. But when Al arrived at the publisher's office, he wasn't alone — the four other members of the group were with him, and they convinced the publisher to give them an instant audition.

The publisher was impressed by what he heard, so impressed that he decided to get the song recorded, and it was apparently released at the end of 1961 on the X label by the group who were billed as the Pendletones, a reference to a brand of windcheater, part of the 'uniform' worn by fashion-conscious surfers. The record created local interest, and in February 1962 was released again, but this time with the names of both the record label and group altered. The label was now Candix, and the group — the Beach Boys, a name suggested by a straightforward Candix publicist, Russ Regan, whose music business talents subsequently carried him to being the president of 20th Century Records.

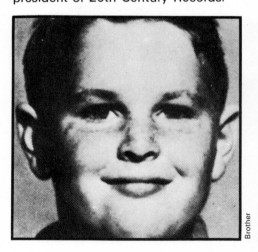

But even *Surfin'* wasn't quite the beginning of a musical career for Brian Wilson, because his father had previously introduced him to Hite Morgan, with whom Brian had made a single under the name of Kenny and the Cadets. Brian was Kenny, the tracks were *Samoa* and *Lone Survivor*, and among the Cadets were Audree Wilson and a friend of Brian's. All we know about it is that it was released on the Dot label in 1961, and that around the same time, Brian produced another single for Dot, with the artist's name given as Rachel and the Revolvers, but both Kenny and Rachel have been lost with the passage of time . . .

Surfin' was definitely not a musical

The Beach Boys' early line-up: left to right, Dennis, David Marks, Carl, Mike Love and Brian.

landmark, except in as much as it was the first record to bear the Beach Boys' name. Some idea of the quality of the song and its recording can be gleaned from Carl's description of the session: "I played basic chords on the guitar, Al thrummed bass, Brian took off his jacket, laid it across the drum and beat it with his hand, while we all sang into one microphone."

This mention of "basic" chords should not be misinterpreted, because while Brian wasn't exactly a virtuoso on any instrument at that point, he had certainly shown a great deal of promise in his musical studies at Hawthorne High School, although his involvement with the Pendletones and his place in the school baseball team tended to divert him from his studies. Part of the musical course which Brian was taking required him to write a sonata, which took the place of a final examination. Instead of the sonata, Brian wrote *Surfin',* and therefore failed the course.

Carl, with rather less high-flown

musical aspirations (he was eventually thrown out of school after failing several examinations, and because he neglected to ask permission to leave in answer to the call of nature), concentrated on learning to play guitar, but even then decided that strict lessons were not what he wanted, and instead moved to a less formal tuition in the company of John Maus. Maus at that time was an average nobody, but it's worth mentioning that he later achieved great fame as John Walker of the Walker Brothers, and in 1963, Carl played live on several occasions with John and Judy, the Maus group of the time.

At this point, Dennis Wilson was more interested in girls and surfing than anything else, so his initial contribution to his brothers' music amounted solely to part time vocalizing, while Mike Love's attempts to learn the saxophone resulted in him playing that instrument with the Beach Boys only occasionally, both because

the instrument was not considered quite appropriate, and because Mike never got around to playing it with any great expertise. Al Jardine, on the other hand, while being the main musician of the group (apparently, the double bass he played was nearly twice his size) was also the first to leave, only a short time after *Surfin'* was released.

It was because Al, or perhaps his parents, felt that he should learn a trade — doubtless, he was influenced by the usual talk of the era about music being at best a hobby, a temporary way of passing the time, but never a career. As Mike Love put it "Al was away for about a year. He had pretensions, ideas of going to a dental school. But he soon figured that he could look down a whole lot more mouths at one time on stage with the Beach Boys than one at a time in a dentist's chair."

The first big gig the Beach Boys played was at Christmas 1961, when they were booked along with a number of other up-and-coming local groups to appear at the Richie Valens Memorial Concert, Valens having died nearly three years before in the same air crash which helped to make Buddy Holly a legend. That gig was apparently the last one before Al went off to learn about teeth, and his replacement was another friend of John Maus, and thus of Carl, one David L. Marks. However, Marks wasn't a bass player like Al, so Brian decided to play that instrument, leaving Marks to perform rhythm guitar duties.

1962 wasn't too old before Candix folded up. *Surfin'* had done reasonably well, but no doubt Candix, being a shoestring type of company, ran out of funds. Later, of course, the tracks that were made for Hite Morgan appeared (and have continued to reappear) on various American compilation albums, the best known of which is probably *The Beach Boys Greatest Hits (1961–1963),* on either the Orbit or Era label, although they do not seem to have been released in Britain – yet.

The ten track album has actually only seven cuts by the Beach Boys – including *Surfin',* plus its B-side, *Luau* – an unconvincing one minute and forty three seconds long, and composed by Hite Morgan in a vain attempt to identify with the surf lyrics which Brian was beginning to write. Morgan also got the group to record two more of his songs, which are banal in the extreme – *Barbee* seems to have been put in a key which the unfortunate vocalist is quite unable to reach, while *What Is A Young Girl* is a kind of third rate Bobby Vee song. Even one of Brian Wilson's own songs, *Judy,* is considerably beneath the peak of his inspiration, and unlike the other three Wilson originals included, has never since seen the light of day. But the other three were quite good in comparison – apart from *Surfin',* they were *Surfin' Safari* and *Surfer Girl.*

After the discovery that no more business could be done with Candix, Murry Wilson took the tracks around to other local record companies, eventually ending up at Capitol Records, where Nik Venet, a house producer, signed the group to the label. "The father had brought a master of their second record, and he wanted to make a new deal," Venet remembered. "He wanted to sell the master, and was asking $100, a small royalty. He didn't want very much . . . a very humble man. I was the only person at the label under 62 – so he played me the record, and it was probably the best record I heard that year, so we bought the master. Gave him $300 for it, and made him a good royalty deal. He wanted to give us the publishing, and I had to advise him to open a small company with the group, split it between them, and keep the publishing."

So the Beach Boys were on Capitol, where they would have a good deal of success before the relationship finally soured . . .

Surfin' Safari

Surfin' Safari was released as a single on Capitol in May 1962, and by November had peaked at number 14 in the national charts. That may seem a long time for a record to be hanging about before it finally makes it, but part of the reason for the delay was that originally *Safari* was the B-side of the record. The original top side had been *409,* a song not about surfing, but hot-rodding, autos being the twin California craze of the time. Apparently, this decision was taken by Nik Venet, who when signing the Beach Boys had usurped Murry as producer. However, it seems that Brian fairly soon afterwards begged his father to get rid of Venet as producer, on the face of it to reinstate his father in that position, but more likely so that he would be able to indulge rather more of his own creative whims without a record company official continually worrying about budgets.

Before further considering the amazing rise of the Beach Boys' career following the entry of *Safari* into the charts, it's amusing to reflect on the changes that have occurred in the pop industry in the years since. In a 1965 concert program, Brian is quoted as saying "This early chapter of Beach Boy history has been buried under a landslide of subsequent smash hits. Before long, it was our forgotten period, but in truth it was the simplest and most uncomplicated rise to popular stardom I've ever known or heard about. Consequently, there is little to talk about our long, hard, bitter struggle for success, which never happened

that way." The program goes on to relate that "The Beach Boy sound fascinated a Capitol veepee [vice president] Voyle Gilmore [in fact, Nik Venet's boss] who inked them for an exclusive Cap wax pact"!

Although the Beach Boys are inextricably intertwined with surf music, Brian Wilson – the man who wrote all those magnificent songs on the subject – has rarely, if ever, ventured near the sea with intent to ride the waves. He even refused to try after his father suggested he should at least go into the water for the sake of the group's image. "I was scared of the water. It *really* scared me." It's ironic that the man who used the slang of surf better than anyone else was only acquiring his information second hand – the album sleeve of *Surfin' Safari* shows the group sitting in a pickup truck (not quite a 'woody', which was an estate wagon with wooden sides, and used by surfers because it was one of the few autos long enough to carry a surf board). All the 'in' terms were relayed to Brian by brother Dennis, the only genuine surfer in the group until Bruce Johnston joined a little later.

It was the same with the car songs. It's not often recognized that there were quite a number of automobile anthems in the Beach Boys' early repertoire. Apart from *409,* the early '60s also produced *Shut Down, Little Deuce Coupe, Our Car Club, Custom Machine, Car Crazy Cutie* and *Cherry Cherry Coupe,* many of which had the lyrics supplied by Roger Christian, a local disc jockey for whom Brian later produced a flop single. With the help of such collaborators, and often with the assistance of Mike Love, Brian Wilson was able to portray the life-style of California in his songs. While his subject matter obviously appealed to Californians, it appealed equally to people on America's East Coast (where surfing didn't happen at all) and in

10

Europe (where you could do it, but where it bore little relationship to the sport as practiced in the Pacific).

Brian's main musical influences had always been located in two areas — he was a great admirer of the finely-crafted harmony singing of the Four Freshman, and to a lesser extent, the Hi-Los, both groups whose work would possibly have been forgotten were it not for the fact that they were so often mentioned in connection with the Beach Boys. To this aspect of his music, Wilson added his other strong influence, the raunchy rock & roll of the '50s, with special reference to the songs of Chuck Berry, who also wrote songs like teenage dream documentaries about car chases, pretty girls and the fantasies which fill the impressionable teenage mind. Brian has never denied his debt to Chuck Berry, although the tie is perhaps more strongly indicated from Berry's side — on a mid-'60s album called *Chuck Berry On Stage,* Berry is introduced by a compere as the writer of *Surfin' USA,* which seems to be stretching things a little, although the opening riff is undoubtedly the Siamese twin of *Sweet Little Sixteen.*

It was very easy for teenage record buyers to identify with the Beach Boys. They attracted an audience that could see itself mirrored in the group's appearance, and who understood exactly what the surf and car songs were all about. While the Beach Boys could hardly claim to have pioneered the wearing of Pendletons, it's very likely that their stage gear, particularly the distinctive striped shirts which they invariably wore until 1966, must have gladdened the hearts of many a clothing manufacturer, and even now that 'uniform' remains the one with which most people instinctively link the group.

After the success of *Surfin' Safari* and the group's resultant popularity, it was time to make an album — naturally called after the hit — and from that album came a track which was the next single, *Ten Little Indians.* It was a complete flop, quite probably because it was about neither hot rods nor surf boards, and the album didn't do much better. But at this time it only took a couple of days to make a record, so during the rest of 1963 the Beach Boys had four more big single hits, but with a reversion to the subject matter which had made them famous. *Surfin' USA* got to number 3 in April, *Surfer Girl,* re-recorded since the Candix sessions, made number 7 in August, and even its B-side, *Little Deuce Coupe,* reached number 15 in September.

But there were changes afoot. Up to this point, Murry Wilson had been a huge influence on his sons, and therefore on the group, but with the assurance that comes with success, the younger Wilsons, and in particular

Brian, began to develop their own ideas about the progress of the Beach Boys. The reasons for this break from the sometimes overwhelming parental discipline were two-fold. First, Wilson Senior was inclined to tyranny at times. In 1962, he went as far as telling Capitol that Mike Love had been fired from the group for swearing backstage — twice! He also would not allow any of the group members to drink alcohol — with the exception of Love, who was legally old enough at 21 — and instituted a system of $500 fines if he caught anyone disobeying this order.

This kind of discipline had applied as much to the Wilson children's early life before the group started. Dennis remembered "My dad was a tyrant. He used to physically beat the crap out of us. His big number was 'Don't ever lie. And if you lie, I'll beat the shit out of you. And if you go outside when it's raining, I'll beat the shit out of you.' So you go outside when it's raining, and you lie to him [about it], and you get hit twice." Taking into consideration the fact that even as a child, Brian was able to make his brothers laugh a lot, but at the wrong times and at the risk of annoying his volatile father, the relationship between father and sons was never gentle. Carl remembered: "We all slept in the same room, and after we went to bed, Brian would sit there trying to make us laugh. First, my mother would come in and warn us. If our father came in, then it was curtains. So we'd be trying not to laugh, covering our mouths, hiding under the sheets, and Brian would keep cracking us up."

Brian's humor was not always directed at those close to him, though, as Dennis recalled: "We'd be rushing to school and Brian would be drinking a carton of milk, and he'd stop and open the door and pretend he was throwing up by emptying out the whole milk carton! Or he'd stop and wait for a hitch-hiker to run up to the car, and then he'd take off!" Dennis also remembered Brian defecating on a plate, and "putting it in front of my dad for dinner!" This last example of Brian's 'humor' was obviously not guaranteed to endear him to his father, and, perhaps, at the age of 21, Brian finally felt himself stifled by the parental control which dominated him.

The second reason for the split was musical development. While Murry Wilson had a background in music, his musical vision was considerably less than that of Brian, who by the end of 1963 had outgrown the simplistic production that had been used on his group's records up to that time.

One of the main stimuli behind this desire to improve the Beach Boys' recorded sound was that Brian had acquired a new musical hero. This was Phil Spector, the man behind the 'wall of sound' productions which made

Gary Usher who co-wrote some of the early songs with Brian.

many hits for artists like the Crystals, the Ronettes and later the Righteous Brothers and Ike and Tina Turner. The final Beach Boys hit of 1963 was probably the first record they made which was obviously Spector-influenced. *Be True To Your School* was much fuller in its backing, with girl singers chanting in the background, and the general impression was that there was a lot going on. Later, of course, Brian progressed as far, or perhaps farther than Spector . . .

One of Spector's most famous quirks was that he never made records in stereo, and here too Brian Wilson had something in common with his idol, for the hearing in one of his ears is extremely inefficient, to the point where he finds it necessary to turn his head to one side at times to hear what is being said to him. As a result, Brian has no alternative but to make his records in mono. "At times, my hearing has hindered me in the studio, because it rings so much, and that's very hard to listen to on a speaker."

No-one seems entirely sure when or how Brian became deaf in his right ear. It has been attributed to a baseball accident, and even to the possibility of a blow from his father in childhood,

Al Jardine (far right) re-joins.

although Murry of course denied this latter posibility. Audree Wilson was asked whether Brian had been born with this defect, but even she didn't know. "Brian thinks it happened when he was around ten," she once told *Rolling Stone*. "Some kid down the street really whacked him in the ear. However, it's a damaged ninth nerve, so he could have been born that way . . . and there's nothing they can do about it."

It seems possible that because of his affliction, Brian perhaps hears sounds in a different way from any other record producer, and as a result, was able to discern flaws in the records he was appearing on, which he wanted to rectify. Thus, the removal of Murry Wilson from the producer's seat may have been brought about by a combination of factors. Of course, had *Surfer Girl,* the remake of which was Brian's first Beach Boys production, not become such a big hit, it's doubtful whether Murry would have allowed him to continue . . .

The result of Brian taking over production duties had wider significance than simply providing his group with a lot of hit records. According to Nik Venet, Brian was a pioneer: "He was one of the first acts on a major label to bust out of the major label syndrome of coming into their studios at their appointed hours and using their facilities, good, bad or indifferent, at their union scales and their hours, changing engineers for dinner breaks, banana breaks, pee breaks, all that bullshit. He was the first one to be allowed to go elsewhere, which was a pretty heavy trip for a kid his age.

"Brian Wilson liberated California for producers and musicians. New York was the center for recording, and he brought a lot of action into California for young producers and musicians. He used guys who were not well known – guys that are called studio cats today at that time were young guys. Brian used them extensively and they became heavy studio cats [because of that]. He also was the first guy to do it until it was right. He damned everybody till it was right, and then he gave them the record – he took his chances. A lot of us would get chicken after four hours, and say 'We'd better get off that tune.' Brian would hang in there for nine hours no matter what the cost. I used to think he was crazy, but he was right."

At the beginning of 1964, Al Jardine re-entered the picture, having had enough of his dental studies. This meant that David Marks was asked to leave the group, although whether or not his departure was willing has never been established. It's also not very clear on which of the group's records Marks played, but his picture appears on several early album sleeves,

those of *Surfin' Safari, Surfin' USA, Surfer Girl* and *Little Deuce Coupe.* This, of course, does not mean that he actually participated in the recording of those albums, and Mike Love *thought* that he was probably on *Surfin' USA, Surfer Girl* and *Shut Down Volume II.* Love also said of Marks: "He is sorely neglected, and unjustly so, for he's a fine gentleman, a nice person, and he has also studied classical music at a music school in Boston. He went from playing rhythm guitar with us to Dave Marks and the Marksmen, a small band in Southern California, then he went east to Boston to study at the conservatory of music. When I last saw him, about 1973 in Boston, he was doing well, feeling good, had grown up very handsomely and nicely, and he wasn't the same snotty punk kid he was when he was in the group!" Marks and his erstwhile colleagues in fact had a reunion in Boston in 1971, but since then little has been heard of him, and after 1963, he no longer played any effective part in the group's history.

Brian Wilson by this time was not confining his activities merely to the Beach Boys. While they were undoubtedly one of the major groups of that particular new wave, there were other recording acts around who were at least as highly considered. One such was Jan and Dean, a duo who had been making teenage type hits since 1958. While they were hardly consistent as a chart act, several singles like *Baby Talk, Heart And Soul* and *Jennie Lee* (the last incompletely credited to Jan and Arnie) had made sufficient impact for the group to be very popular in California.

At one point in those early days, the Beach Boys played a concert as Jan and Dean's support act, in many ways a crucial meeting for both groups, as Dean Torrence remembers: "When *Surfin'* came out, we heard it and liked it. We weren't afraid of it at all, in fact I think we sensed that it was going to help, that it would be good for business – it would be good to have more California groups, because we didn't have that many out here. But I think what really did it was a concert that we did with them right after *Surfin'.* I think they'd recorded *Surfin' Safari,* and it had just been out a couple of weeks, and had got a lot of plays, so we were familiar with it. We did this concert together, and they were to back us, so we met in a house trailer, where we changed, plus we sat around and taught them our repertoire of four songs. They came out and did their two songs and a couple of instrumentals, and then we came out and did our three or four songs – I don't think we had many that we could do live! When we'd done our set, the crowd was really excited, an excitement that we'd never really felt before, because it was a male audience

15

Jan Berry and Dean Torrence: 'Surf City' was Brian's first number 1.

as well as a female audience for the first time. Really nice, a bigger mass of people out there.

"So after we finished our three songs, which had nothing particularly to do with surfing, we realized that they wanted more, so we asked the Beach Boys 'Hey, do you want to do your set again, and we'll sing with you guys?', because we all knew the parts, easy parts, and in fact we could do some of the parts they couldn't do. So they said 'Gee, you'll sing *our* songs?', and I said 'Sure, I think your songs are really fun to sing.' So we sang *Surfin'* and *Surfin' Safari*, and really had a ball singing them. And we really listened to those parts that Brian was writing — they sounded simple, but they were really great. I remember driving home after that, and saying 'Man, those parts are really good, they're really fun to sing. Maybe we should give Brian a call next week and see if he's got any tunes.'

"But the next thing that happened was that we were caught right in the middle of thinking about surfing — but the Four Seasons had just happened too. We had done a record called *Linda,* which was a direct steal of the

Four Seasons and was a big hit. So we had *Linda,* yet we wanted to do surfing, and somebody, probably Lou Adler, said 'Why don't you take Linda surfing, and do an album called *Jan And Dean Take Linda Surfing.* That gets it all in there.' So we agreed to that, except that we didn't know any surfing songs except the two that the Beach Boys had done. So we called up Brian and said 'Brian, we've got a hit record with *Linda,* we're going to do an album with a fairly good budget, but we need your help. Would you come on in and play the tracks for us to *Surfin'* and *Surfin' Safari,* and we'll put them on our album.'

"He was just totally knocked out that we were going to record his songs! He said 'Sure, I'll get the guys,' and all of them showed up at the studio, and we got re-introduced to one another, and sat around drinking beer and stuff and they played the two tracks, sang all the background parts with us. We sang essentially what we sang on stage that one night. Then Brian showed us stuff he'd been doing, like dualing voices and even dualing background vocals. We were used to dualing leads and maybe fal-

settos, but never the four parts, and he showed us how to do the four parts over again. And that was it, that was really the key to the whole thing. Then, of course, right after that we said 'Now that we've got those two songs, do you have any new ones that you're working on?' And he played a song called *(When Summer Comes) Gonna Hustle You,* which I always loved, and I thought was a smash. We were sitting there, saying 'That's great! We'll take it — do you have anything more?', and he had a song that was half finished, and he showed us the chords and stuff, and we took it away, and in the next couple of weeks we finished it, putting all the lyrics in that he hadn't finished."

Surf Music—The New Wave

That song was *Surf City*, not only the biggest single that Jan and Dean ever released, selling over one and a quarter million copies, but also the first surf record to reach number 1 in the charts, in August 1963.

Another of Brian's recording projects at the time revolved around the lady singers who had appeared to great effect on *Be True To Your School* at the end of 1963. The girls were Marilyn and Diane Rovell, and their cousin Ginger Blake. Ginger knew Gary Usher, another songwriting partner of Brian Wilson, and she took Marilyn along to a club in Los Angeles to hear the Beach Boys playing *Surfin' Safari*. The story goes that Brian looked down from the stage to see Marilyn drinking a cup of hot chocolate, whereupon he asked if he could share it with her. When she obliged, Brian managed to spill it on her. That was in 1962, when Marilyn was only 14 years old and Brian was apparently engaged at the time . . .

During the next couple of years, Brian and the three girls became good friends. He wrote some songs for them, and recommended them to Nik Venet, who produced their first single, *Surfin' Down The Swanee River,* a gentle rewrite of the familiar *Swanee River,* for which Brian took the songwriting credit. It was a stiff, as were the other two releases in 1963 by the Honeys (the name the girls adopted) but Brian remained interested in them, and especially in Marilyn, who was to play a major part in his future.

Meanwhile, the Beach Boys were doing very well in America, although their 1963 Christmas single *Little Saint Nick,* backed by a lush harmony version of The Lord's Prayer, was not a great success. In Britain, the group were virtually unknown still — only *Surfin' Safari, Ten Little Indians* and *Surfin' USA* had been released there, and you had to be exceedingly hip to have even heard of the group, let alone possess their records. Strangely enough, the same was true, to a certain extent, in America because as far as the album market went, the Beach Boys were somewhat obscure.

The *Surfin' Safari* album had been released at the end of 1962, but as it largely consisted of fillers, it didn't become in demand until it was difficult to get. Much the same was true of the *Surfin' USA* album, released in the spring of 1963 in America. It contained the hit single as the title track, plus the B-side, *Shut Down,* and ten other tracks, most of which are so obscure and mediocre that few people wanted them.

The efforts to get this record into the charts weren't helped by Capitol simultaneously releasing a bizarre compilation album called *Shut Down.* This contained a couple of the Beach Boys car songs – the title track and *409* – plus a number of other tracks by other people loosely connected with hot rods and allied subjects, like *Black Denim Trousers And Motorcycle Boots, Four On The Floor* and *Hot Rod Race.* However, probably the most curious items included are *Brontosaurus Stomp,* the B-side to the Piltdown Men's hit *McDonald's Cave* (the Piltdown Men were rumored to be the session musicians who played on the then much-acclaimed Frank Sinatra LPs for Capitol), and a track by Robert Mitchum, of all people, singing (loosely) *The Ballad Of Thunder Road.* Some people purchased the *Shut Down* album, under the impression that it was by the Beach Boys. Disappointment on finding the truth was great and the group must have lost a great many fans. It was to be the first of many items which could cause bad feeling between the Beach Boys and Capitol Records.

Another similar example came six months later, in September 1963. A *Surfer Girl* album was released, with a number of new and reasonably substantial songs, like *Catch A Wave, In My Room* and *Hawaii.* Obviously, the album was put out to capitalize on the fact that the title track was a hit, and included the B-side of the single – the excellent *Little Deuce Coupe.* But when *Coupe* itself became a hit, Capitol put out another LP only a few weeks later under that title!

By this time, even the most unobservant Beach Boys fan would have noticed that the group's LPs contained a good deal of duplication. *409* had already appeared on three different albums, both *Little Deuce Coupe* and *Shut Down* on two, and the group had ostensibly had four albums released in one year! Not only was this an undesirable thing artistically (surely the group must have reflected on the possibility that Capitol were treating them as a flash in the pan, shoveling vinyl into the shops while they could still be called stars), but the speed

Capitol

The boys' biggest movie role was 'Girls On The Beach' in 1964.

with which it was necessary to make these albums inevitably resulted in the quality of the songs being poor. Murry Wilson was a witness to the speed with which the albums were made: "At Western Recorders, I remember they stood and sang for 13 hours – 13 hours straight – to get the *Surfin' USA* album out." It seems quite likely that at the end of 1963, the Beach Boys were getting famous – but they were getting equally tired.

Early 1964 saw a great deal of progress for the group, particularly as regards their being recognized outside the States. The first single of the year was another which owed a debt to Chuck Berry, *Fun, Fun, Fun,* an enduring anthem of a girl who 'borrows' her father's Thunderbird car to go cruising for burgers, instead of to the library, under which pretext she had been allowed to use the car. It's a brilliant song, and illustrates the incredible command of the Californian teen culture possessed by Brian and Mike Love, who co-wrote the song.

The girls can't stand her, 'cause she walks, looks and drives like an ace, now.
She makes the "Indy" five hundred

Capitol

'The T.A.M.I. Show' (above). Right: 'The Monkey's Uncle'.

look like a Roman chariot race now. A lotta guys try to catch her but she leads them on a wild goose chase now. And she'll have fun, fun, fun, till her daddy takes the T-bird away.

The record started with a ripped off guitar passage straight from Berry's *Johnny B. Goode,* and it should be noted that while Chuck Berry was past his first peak in America, in Britain the Beatles and the Rolling Stones were just reintroducing most of Berry's early work to a new generation. *Fun, Fun, Fun* was a revelation — for Britain, it was one of the few worthwhile American records to come out in that year (and it was a year which boasted such excitements as a slew of Jim Reeves hits and *Hello Dolly* by Louis Armstrong), while America was reeling under the onslaught of the British Invasion. For the first time, British-made records held the number 1 position in the charts for longer than Americans, with the Beatles, Peter and Gordon, the Animals and Manfred Mann all getting to the top. The only act who seemed unconcerned were the Beach Boys, who achieved another four hits that year, and were probably the only pre-invasion American group

to successfully survive the British beat holocaust.

Fun, Fun, Fun got to number 5 in the US charts, but wasn't a hit in Britain, although it turned a lot of heads. However, the next single, *I Get Around* was a top tenner in both countries – number 1 in the States – no doubt helped along in the UK by the fact that the Rolling Stones recommended it on the most popular TV show of the time, *Ready, Steady, Go!* As a result, a flood of Beach Boys albums began to be released in Britain – previously, there had been four singles and a couple of EPs, but when *I Get Around* took off, there was a Beach Boys album released every few weeks. Those first two singles of 1964 raised the group to a plateau from which they've never really fallen – they were among the ten biggest groups in the world.

But despite its promising beginning, 1964 wasn't all fun, fun, fun for the group. There were stirrings of unrest throughout the year. Mike Love explained one bone of contention, "Just because a certain style sells in one year, it's not necessarily going to sell in the next. We'd moved on, evolved and changed – witness the first verse of *I Get Around* – 'I'm getting *bugged* driving up and down the same old strip, I've got to find a *new* place where the kids are *hip*,' hip meaning awareness." Certainly, it seems that Brian and Mike were finding no challenge in turning out songs very quickly – apparently they wrote *Fun, Fun, Fun,* for instance, in a taxi while traveling between the Holiday Inn and the airport in Salt Lake City.

The disenchantment with the subject matter of their songs was of little consequence compared with what was to happen by the end of that year. Two major upsets occurred, the first of which concerned Murry Wilson, who was removed from the management of his sons' group at their instigation. Brian explained it to an American correspondent of Britain's *New Musical Express* at the time: "We changed from our father to outside management basically because of the emotional strain we were under. We didn't feel that we were driving for the things we should have been since we are in a golden position to progress, and become possibly more successful. We felt that even though my father had his heart behind it and had good intentions, because of the situation you get into between father and son, you just seem to go nowhere. It's an emotional struggle, and that's more or less a crippled situation so we eliminated it. It was done more or less maturely. Finally, we decided he is better as a father, not a manager."

Murry's wife Audree also remembered that time and told *Rolling Stone* "It destroyed Murry, but I understood perfectly why they did it. He was

destroyed by that, and yet he wasn't really up to it. He'd already had an ulcer, and it was really too much for him, but he loved them so much. He was overly protective really, he couldn't let them go. He couldn't stand seeing anyone else handling his kids."

A less kindly viewpoint is that of Nik Venet, who said "I used to get locked up in the office with the man. I was into all kinds of great things, and the next morning I would have to come to work at 9 o'clock after being up all night with great music. And I would walk into that office, and there would be Murry Wilson. He'd sit there till 5 or 6 o'clock and tell me about his songs and play me his melodies, and I had to listen to him because somewhere in the conversation he would always drop to me what Brian's next record was gonna be . . . I was stuck with him, 'cause I was the producer. The father kept trying to worm his way into a recording deal, and eventually he made one with Capitol, which is hilarious! Capitol made a whole album and released it . . . just so they could satisfy him and so he wouldn't hassle them so much on some of the Beach Boys things."

That album *The Many Moods Of Murry Wilson*, has been described by people who have heard it as "pathetic," and while one should not speak ill of the dead, the underlying question about Murry Wilson's management of the Beach Boys has to relate to whether his eventual motive in representing

his sons was purely for their good, or in part for self-gratification, including the release of that LP. In fairness to him, since that time the Beach Boys have been through quite a number of managers and representatives . . .

While firing your own father must be a traumatic event, something far more serious occurred at the end of 1964, by which time the group's vinyl score had increased considerably. Two more American hits had been released – *When I Grow Up To Be A Man* and *Dance, Dance, Dance.* Both nestled into the US Top 10 at the end of the year, although another Christmas single, *The Man With All The Toys,* was no more successful than the previous year's *Little Saint Nick.* In addition, a lot more albums came out pegged to hit singles – *Shut Down Volume II* was totally by the Beach Boys, unlike its earlier namesake, and led off with *Fun, Fun, Fun,* while *All Summer Long* started with *I Get Around.* Both contained several of the minor classics which have become latterday Beach Boys standards like *Don't Worry Baby, The Warmth Of The Sun, All Summer Long, Wendy, Little Honda* (apparently the only Beach Boys motorcycle song) and *Girls On The Beach.* This last track, in fact, was written for the '64 beach movie of the same name which featured the Beach Boys playing many of the songs that eventually appeared on the album *All Summer Long.* Other movie appearances in '64 included the

opening dance sequence of Disney's *The Monkey's Uncle* and the first filmed rock concert, *The T.A.M.I. Show* (also known as *Gather No Moss* or *Teenage Command Performance*). At the end of the year, *The Beach Boys Christmas Album* was released (now a much-in-demand collector's item), plus a live album, *The Beach Boys' Concert.*

All this activity was having a taxing effect on Brian Wilson, and culminated in a nervous breakdown on an airplane trip to Houston on December 23, 1964. "I was run down mentally and emotionally because I was running around, jumping on jets from one city to another on one night stands, also producing, writing, arranging, singing, planning, teaching, to the point where I had no peace of mind and no chance to actually sit down and rest or think. I was so mixed up and so overworked. We were going to Houston to kick off a two-week tour. I said goodbye to Marilyn — we weren't getting along too good. The plane had only been in the air five minutes when I told Al Jardine I was going to crack up any minute, but he told me to cool it. Then I started crying, I put a pillow over my face and began screaming and yelling, and I started telling people I wasn't getting off the plane. I was getting far out, coming undone, having a breakdown, and I just let myself go completely. The rubber band had stretched as far as it would go."

Apart from what Brian had to say

The Boys visit the UK to appear on the TV show 'Ready, Steady, Go!' Right: Brian greeted by a fan at London's Heathrow Airport.

about overwork, there are a number of other possible contributory factors to his breakdown. Seemingly, his bad ear had been troubling him rather more than usual, no doubt as a result of being exposed to large, very loud PA systems such as would fill huge halls. Also, it seems that Brian was in love — with Marilyn Rovell. "We were like girlfriend and boyfriend for a year and a half," she told *Rolling Stone*. "I was already totally in love with him, you know — and yet he would never admit that there were feelings for me. The time that he did do it, the guys were going to Australia and I remember sitting in the airport with Brian and Mike, and Mike goes 'Wow, Brian boy, we're sure going to have a good time in Australia.' And Brian's kind of looking at me from the corner of his eye, and he's going 'Yeah, we are, aren't we.' And I can't imagine why I said this, but I just went 'That's great, because I'm going to have a good time too.' You know, the typical childish things. And Brian looked at me like — the first time I ever saw such an expression on his face — like, 'What? What'd you say?' Anyway, they went on a plane for 13 hours, and that night, when they arrived in Australia, I got the call from him. Two telegrams had come in the meantime. I got the call, and for the first time he called me 'honey'."

He also told Marilyn he wanted her to be his wife, and on the group's return from that tour, he and she were married, in December 1964, just a short time before that first breakdown. Of course, it's very natural for a newly-wed to want to spend a lot of his time with his wife, and what with that and the other pressures Brian was having to bear, a nervous breakdown was almost a predictable result. After that, Brian's doctors advised him that continual touring might drive him to severe ill health, as well as affecting his good (left) ear. There was only one thing to be done — Brian had to stop performing live with the group he had masterminded to enormous success.

However, the information that a replacement was going to be necessary remained Brian's secret for a few more weeks. He didn't tell the rest of the group until they were in the studio completing what was to be the *Beach Boys Today* album, and their reaction was predictably disturbed. "They all broke down. I'd already gone through my breakdown — now it was their turn. Mike had a couple of tears in his eyes. He couldn't take the reality that their big brother wasn't ever going to be on the stage with them again. It was a blow to their sense of security, of course. Mike lost his cool, and felt like there was no reason to go on. Dennis picked up a big ashtray and told some people to get out of there or he'd hit them on the head with it. Al Jardine broke out in tears and stomach cramps. He was all goofed up and my mother,

24

who was there, had to take care of him. And good old Carl was the only guy who never got into a bad emotional scene. He just sat there and didn't get uptight about it — he always kept a cool head. If it weren't for Carl, it's hard to say where we'd be, and he cooled Dennis, Mike and Al down. Now it was just a matter of time until the guys adjusted to the new scene. The first replacement we had was Glen Campbell. He was adequate, but he wasn't really a Beach Boy, he didn't look or act like one."

Yes, that's the very same Glen Campbell who today is every house-wife's dream and regularly appears on the television singing bland ballads. At that time, in early 1965, Glen was better known as a hot session guitarist than a singer, but his stay with the Beach Boys was brief. "That must have gone on for three or four months, then Glen got sick and couldn't tour. The Beach Boys were really in trouble, because they couldn't cancel out the tour, so Mike at the last minute called up Bruce Johnston, and found that he was free. Bruce and Carl got together, and Carl taught him all the songs we were doing together on stage, and Bruce learned enough songs in one day to perform with the group the next night. In one day's practice, he got into the Beach Boys."

Bruce Johnston joined the Beach Boys on April 9, 1965. Although this was his first time in a topline band, he'd had plenty of surf music experience in California. He'd played around Los Angeles with the Rip Chords *(Hey Little Cobra)* and a duo called Bruce and Terry *(Summer Means Fun)*. Terry was Terry Melcher — son of Doris Day — who really excelled as a producer and was later responsible for the Byrds' early recordings, including *Mr Tambourine Man*. Brian's withdrawal from the group left a further gap, one that Carl filled. The Beach Boys needed a leader and spokesman — roles that the dominant Brian had filled — and as Carl was the only one who had taken the upheaval calmly, he seemed the natural replacement.

The album which was being made when the fuss started, *Beach Boys Today*, came out in March 1965, and produced three hits — *Dance, Dance, Dance, Do You Wanna Dance*, a remake of the old Bobby Freeman song of the '50s, and another number 1, *Help Me Rhonda*. The next album, *Summer Days (And Summer Nights)* saw an increasing awareness by the group that they should progress. People were beginning to treat the group as past it. As Carl said "There was a time when it was uncool to be into the Beach Boys, and when we did that album, it started to bother us, doing this same stuff, because we thought we were trapped into having

'The Christmas Album' publicity.

Capitol

to sing about a certain thing." And by now the group's growing disenchantment with Capitol wasn't making them any happier.

Nevertheless, that album, which saw Bruce's recording debut (uncredited because he was still contracted to CBS) with the group on the wonderful *California Girls,* conformed fairly well to the patterns previously laid down. *California Girls* was a huge success, getting to number 3 in August 1965. *The Little Girl I Once Knew* was their first hit of 1966, while they achieved more gold discs for million dollar albums than any US group in 1965. There were five albums which reached the magic figure, but that might never have happened if Capitol weren't flooding the market with Beach Boys albums.

There was to be one more hit before the bubble finally burst. Late in 1965, it was decided that the Beach Boys would make an album called *Beach Boys' Party.* As luck would have it, while it was being recorded, Jan and Dean were in the same building, making a song called *You Really Know How To Hurt A Guy.* Dean loathed the song, to such an extent that he refused to sing on it, and instead went down the hall to where the *Party* album was being made. "They were all sitting around drunk trying to think of another song to do, and they asked me what I wanted to sing. When they told me what they'd sung already, I suggested *Barbara-Ann,* and they said 'OK'. We tried a few times, and changed keys, and then started, and that's exactly how it happened. I sang it, and spent about 20 minutes there drinking and eating, and then I went back to our studio. Jan said 'Did you sing with them?' and I said 'Yeah, on *Barbara-Ann.*' He said 'Oh, that could never be a hit again,' and I said 'So who wants hits? It's just an album cut, why are you talking about a hit?' He used to get really uptight like that, very jealous."

As luck would have it, that was the track which Capitol selected as the single from the *Party* album, and it got to number 2 in the States, and was the Beach Boys' biggest hit in Britain thus far, at number 3. Unfortunately, due to record company politics, which had prevented Jan and Dean and the Beach Boys from forming what might have been a highly successful collaboration, Dean wasn't permitted to be credited on the album or single, but at the very end of the track, Carl's voice can be heard saying something like "Thank you, Dean." It was one way to repay an earlier debt, because on Jan and Dean's *Surf City* hit, Dean has claimed that he could always hear much more of Brian's voice than Jan's. Problems with record companies were becoming a strain which would have an increasing impact on the Beach Boys.

The Golden Years
1966-67

Bruce Johnston joins (far left).

The *Beach Boys' Party* album, as usual a great commercial success, left the group at a crossroads. They were still generally considered to be a surfing group, although the description was appealing to them less and less. But in some ways it would have been foolish to throw away the advantage gained from the long and continuous array of hits. The single from the *Party* album, *Barbara-Ann,* had screamed up the singles chart, although only Capitol — not the group — had any faith in it.

Apparently, the public didn't want the Beach Boys to change, and they further demonstrated that fact by buying *Beach Boys' Party* in sufficient amounts for it to qualify for a gold record. Strangely, especially in view of the esteem in which the Beach Boys are currently held, it was to be their last gold LP for eight years! Such a statistic is still more bizarre when one considers that the next LP released by the group, *Pet Sounds,* is without doubt their best known and most praised album.

Pet Sounds

Around the beginning of 1966, the Beach Boys, without Brian Wilson, went to Japan for a tour — pictures of them there form a collage on the back of the *Pet Sounds* sleeve. They left Brian behind both in order that he could begin work on the new album, and also because his health was still not good enough to withstand the rigors of a tour, even in a non-playing capacity. But that wasn't his only problem — Capitol Records wanted some more big sellers using the old formula, but Brian was trying to progress. "I've never written one note or word of music simply because I think it will make money," he said.

An added spur to his ambition was the remarkable new music that was appearing at that time, produced by his contemporaries. The Lovin' Spoonful, the Mamas and Papas, the Association and Simon and Garfunkel all made a tremendous impact in 1966 — and of course the Stones and the Beatles were moving into more diverse directions, with records like *Eleanor Rigby* and *Paint It Black.*

Brian Wilson has frequently been cited as a man who works best when the competition is at its strongest, and with *Pet Sounds,* he certainly proved that to be true. Carl Wilson has said that at some points in the '60s it wasn't done to be a Beach Boys fan, but that all changed with *Pet Sounds* — although the other members of the group were certainly not as happy with the album as Brian when they first heard it. By the time they returned from Japan, a good deal of the instrumental

work on the album had been done, as usual, by session musicians. But in a more musically trail-blazing style than previously, which startled the rest of the group. It's interesting to reflect on Bruce Johnston's thoughts on that subject much more recently — "If someone can do it better, get them! Because the Beach Boys thing is singing, even though everyone can play." It was not always so.

Capitol Records weren't too pleased with *Pet Sounds* either. Having proved to be right in releasing *Barbara-Ann* they felt, justifiably enough, that they knew what an acceptable Beach Boys sound was — and *Pet Sounds* was certainly not acceptable to them, no doubt because it contains a subtlety lacking in surf and hot rod songs. In fact, Capitol showed their displeasure by refusing to release the new album, and when they were finally convinced (by the threat that Brian might not ever make records for them again), they completely refused to promote the record.

In *Crawdaddy* magazine, Timothy White explained what this momentous album meant to Brian Wilson. "It was to be his bid for acceptance as an artist. He had become increasingly obsessed with the notion that the All-American Beach Boys, and those Liverpool interlopers, the Beatles, were locked into some strange, slightly sinister Battle of the Titans being staged on the US record charts. From 1964 on, the two groups' singles see-sawed wildly in the Top 20, with the Beatles usually winning out. It was a situation that caused Brian some mild consternation when the British band broke big in the States, but he became downright distressed after his health compelled the retreat into the control room."

The turning point was apparently the Beatles' *Rubber Soul* LP, which Brian recognizes as a genuinely complete work, without any filler, and arguably, although the term fell out of favor, a concept album. Of course, it has been claimed that Brian himself had made concept albums before — such as the wall-to-wall car album *Little Deuce Coupe.* But the Beatles were not simply stringing a dozen similar songs together — by some genius they were putting on one disc a series of compositions which really seemed to belong together. When Brian heard *Rubber Soul,* he determined to at least equal it, if not improve on it, one reason why a good deal more time and trouble was spent on *Pet Sounds* than on any previous album.

Despite the lack of recognition in terms of sales, *Pet Sounds* has evoked more quotes about it than anything the Beach Boys have done before or since. Richard Williams in *Melody Maker* provides a more readable commentary than most: "It was immedi-

ately obvious that Brian had traveled further than anyone in popular music, extended its scope beyond a fantasist's wildest dreams. *Pet Sounds* was a massive elaboration on the more interesting aspects of his earlier work; the harmonies were denser, structured in myriad layers, achingly lush, yet . . . pure. The words (mostly by advertising man Tony Asher) assumed a newly mature view of emotional relationships . . . but it was the arrangements which blew minds. Brian had used a bewildering array of resources, more than Spector and the equally iconoclastic Burt Bacharach combined.''

Even before the album was ready, a hit single emerged, although few think of *Sloop John B* – a remake of an old folk song – as being one of the high points of the album. (The song had been a hit in England for Lonnie Donegan in 1960 under the title *I Wanna Go Home*.) The single, probably the nearest thing on the album to the 'old' Beach Boys sound, and presumably chosen by Capitol as the single for that very reason, made the Top 3 in both Britain and America and credit should be given to the group's token folkie, Al Jardine, for providing the idea behind it. Everybody was pleased that the record was a hit, because an unsuccessful single had previously been released, *Caroline, No,* credited not to the Beach Boys, but to

Brian Wilson, which had flopped, although in retrospect, its superiority to *Sloop John B* is staggering.

The album also produced more bona fide classics than any other Beach Boys album – apart from the tracks already mentioned, *God Only Knows, Wouldn't It Be Nice* and *Here Today* rank among Brian Wilson's very best songs. The first two were hits, although a strange story surrounds *God Only Knows*. Probably the premier British surf-type group of the time were Tony Rivers and the Castaways. They were assured that the Beach Boys were definitely not going to release *God Only Knows* as a single in the UK, so they swiftly produced a cover version of reasonable accuracy, which entered the bottom of the chart. However, it seems that no-one had told Capitol about this promise, and very soon a Beach Boys version rushed up to number 2, completely obliterating the Rivers version. Another British group, Robb Storme and the Whispers, produced an unsuccessful cover version of *Here Today,* indicating that the Beach Boys were now in the top echelon of groups with each new album spawning British copyists, something which had only previously happened regularly to the Beatles and the Rolling Stones, since the start of the British beat boom.

It has been suggested that the in-

spiration, if that's the word, behind much of the material on *Pet Sounds* resulted from Brian and Marilyn's recurring marital problems; certainly there is a wistful quality about a number of the songs. Witness: ''God only knows what I'd be without you,'' or ''Wouldn't it be nice if we were married, then we wouldn't have to wait so long?'' and ''Love is here today and gone tomorrow'' – all have the same teen appeal as before, but are couched in far more complex surroundings. Perhaps his own problems were making Brian more reflective, as Dennis Wilson remembered: ''My father used to go to pieces when he heard stuff like *Caroline, No.* See, a lot of people didn't know it, but that song was about a girl that Brian was really in love with in high school, named Caroline. He saw her again years later, and it all came back to him, and he wrote the song.''

This was also the period when one of Brian Wilson's most publicized bouts of 'eccentricity' started and he installed a sandbox in the room where he wrote his music, with his piano carefully placed in the sand. Marilyn Wilson didn't think it was such an odd idea, she said in *Rolling Stone:* ''Well, he wanted a sandbox, so he got a sandbox. I mean, who am I to tell a creator what he can do? He said 'I want to play in the sand, I want to feel like a little kid. When I'm writing these songs, I want to feel what I'm writing, all the happiness.'" Perhaps this was an unconscious reversion on Brian's part to his childhood, when there were few aggravations in his personal life. A time when there were no hassles in his professional relationship with a record company who still wanted him to stand in the same musical position he'd occupied for five years.

"Brian wanted to experience it all," said Marilyn. "So he had this really good carpenter come up to the house, and in the dining room the guy built a gorgeous wood sandbox, around two and a half feet tall. And then they came with a dump truck and dumped eight tons of sand in it. I have the funniest story about the piano tuner — he walked into the house, and the sandbox had been there for a while, and I was very used to it. He says 'OK, where's the piano?', and I was busy in the house, and I said 'Oh, it's over there in the sandbox,' thinking nothing of it. He looks at me, and walks over to the sandbox and sits down, and starts taking off his shoes and socks! That made me roar! And the sand, being there is no sun, is freezing cold. By the way, the dogs had also used it — you know, dogs and sand . . ."

Although the installation of a box of sand in your living room may seem a little excessive, there's no doubt that the various problems assailing him, together with an intense desire to compete with the Beatles, were driving Brian Wilson to go beyond the previous boundaries he'd met. Marilyn: "He just told me one night, he said 'Marilyn, I'm gonna make the greatest album, the greatest rock album ever made,' and he meant it. Boy, he worked his butt off when he was making *Pet Sounds.* And I'll never forget the night that he got the final disc, when it was finished. We went in the bedroom where we had a stereo, and we just lay there all night on the bed, and just listened and cried and did a whole thing. But *Pet Sounds* was not a big hit. That really hurt him badly, he couldn't understand it. It's like, why put your heart and soul into something?"

Certainly everyone connected with the album still regards it as something very special. Bruce Johnston, whose first complete Beach Boys album it was, remains effusive about it years later: "I think that album is my favorite, and it drove me crazy that I couldn't get my picture on the cover because I was still signed to CBS, from the days when Terry Melcher and I were producing for them. I couldn't get a clearance to be on the front of the cover, but I'm on the back." Although it's pretty difficult to recognize the faces in many of the photographs because they're fairly small and, in several, the group are made up to look Japanese. "But I'm so proud just to have been

able to sing on that record . . ."

At the end of 1976, in an interview on a New York radio show, Brian was asked which were the songs from the entire Beach Boys repertoire that revealed the most about him. He replied: "I think *That's Not Me* from *Pet Sounds* reveals a lot about myself . . . just the idea that you're going to look at yourself, and say 'Hey, that's not me.' You're going to get your identity clear, kind of square off with yourself, say this is me, that's not me. That explains it. I think *God Only Knows* explains a lot about me in that I believe in God, and I am humble enough to say God knows what I would be without whoever I was talking about. Or say I was talking about an imaginary person, which I was at that time. But it just goes to show feelings. When you believe in something you reflect it in your songs, you say how you feel, and songs don't lie. Songs are the most honest form of human being there is — there's nothing that lies about a song."

It's amazing, in retrospect, to recall that America was deaf to *Pet Sounds.* In Britain, just for a pleasant change, the LP was treated with the respect that it deserved, getting to number 2 in the album charts, and staying in the Top 10 for six months. But in the States the record was to all intents and purposes ignored, even when it was

later reissued as a bonus album, at no extra cost, with the *Carl And The Passions* album during the early '70s. Carl has also always been convinced that *Pet Sounds* deserves a special place in rock history. "A lot of people say *Sgt Pepper* was the first concept album, but the truth is that *Pet Sounds* was really the first. It was thematic musically." Just over a year after the Beach Boys album came out, the Beatles released *Sgt Pepper,* and any remaining hope Brian Wilson might have had left for public acceptance of his masterwork (although critical opinion everywhere, including in America, had been universally in favor) vanished.

Perhaps we should leave the last word on the subject to Murry Wilson. "*Pet Sounds* is a masterpiece of accomplishment for Brian, although the public doesn't realize it, most of them, but Brian took a lot of the masters, approached the music in his own way, and put a rock & roll beat to it. He even got Stephen Foster in there — phrases that we used to sing when he was a baby, you know? And it's twisted around with his beautiful approach to rock & roll, and his bass root; his bass root figurations of the bass guitar are quite fantastic! *Pet Sounds* has been copied, chewed up, renewed — Negro artists have used it in band arrangements, commercials have used

Capitol

it. Every day you hear a commercial that has a Beach Boys sound in back of it.'' For once, paternal pride in a son was truly vindicated, although regrettably not by the record buyers of America.

Because Brian Wilson's masterpiece was not received with the acclaim it deserved (and which its creator expected) — something that can only be due to ignorance on the part of the American consumer — there was to be a shortage of new Beach Boys records for about a year. It had less impact on Capitol Records than might have been expected, because shortly after *Pet Sounds* had failed to sell in vast quantities, *Best Of The Beach Boys* came out — a collection easily able to bridge a couple of years' gap in potential sales. Interestingly, the British version was different (and superior) to its American counterpart. While the US version had 12 tracks, the UK one had 14, and only five tracks were common to both records. But that didn't stop either of them selling . . .

Good Vibrations

Brian Wilson's quandary as to what his next move should be resulted in him taking a reported six months to make his next single, which was the song that most Beach Boys fans, and many others besides, consider to be the greatest single record ever made. The track, of course, was *Good Vibrations,* and rumors persist that it had originally been scheduled for inclusion on *Pet Sounds,* although in a very different form from the one we all know and love. There was even some talk of Brian having despaired of the song, and having wanted to give it to a black vocal group to record.

Fortunately he was talked out of that and continued with a creative process which once more created new frontiers in rock music. For example, an instrument called the theremin is used, providing the unworldly sound which can be best heard at the end of the record. Apparently, the idea for using this sound came to Brian after he had watched a Bette Davis horror film, and it seems that his imaginative production has effectively prevented just about everyone else in rock from using the instrument, which is a simple type of synthesizer.

Such innovatory work made a number of critics suggest that had Brian been born in an earlier time, he might have been challenging the likes of Beethoven, although, in truth, this is nonsense. However, Brian is supposed to have said ''I wanted to see what I was capable of doing. I tried to reach a personal pinnacle of writing, arranging and producing with *Good Vibrations.*'' Of course, such lofty statements could easily have been a defence for

the rumored $16,000 that the single cost to make . . .

In a 1976 issue of *Rolling Stone,* Brian spoke at length about the song. ''It took six months to make. We recorded the very first part of it at Gold Star Recording Studio, then we took it to a place called Western, then to Sunset Sound, and then to Columbia. We wanted to experiment using four different studio sounds — every studio has its own marked sound. Using the four studios had a lot to do with the way the final record sounded. So it took quite a while. There's a story behind this record — my mother used to tell me about vibrations, and I didn't really understand too much of what she meant when I was a boy. It scared me, the word 'vibrations' — to think that invisible feelings, invisible vibrations existed scared me to death. But she told about dogs that would bark at people, but wouldn't bark at others, that a dog would pick up vibrations from some people that you can't see, but you can feel. And the same thing happened with people.

''So we talked about good vibrations, and experimented with the song and the idea, and we decided that on the one hand you could say:

I love the colorful clothes she wears, and the way the sunlight plays upon her hair.
I hear the sound of a gentle word on the wind that lifts her perfume through the air.

Those are sensual things. And then you say 'I'm pickin' up good vibrations,' which is a contrast against the sensual, the extra-sensory perception that we have. That's what we're really talking about. *Good Vibrations* was advanced rhythm & blues music, but we took a great risk. As a matter of fact, I didn't think it was going to make it because of its complexity, but apparently people accepted it very well. They felt that it had a naturalness to it, it flowed.''

When he had finally finished the track, Brian was very pleased with it, as he had every right to be. In direct contrast to their rejection of the magnificent *Pet Sounds,* the public took *Good Vibrations* to their hearts, and it remains the best selling single that the Beach Boys have released, reaching number 1 on both sides of the Atlantic just before Christmas 1966. ''I felt that it was a plateau. First of all, it felt very arty, and it sounded arty. Second, it was the first utilization of a cello in rock & roll music to that extent, using it as an upfront instrument, as a rock instrument.''

The man Brian got to help him out with the arrangements for the cello was to play a significant part in the next year-long chapter of the Beach Boys' career. His name was Van Dyke Parks, and after the excitement

caused by *Good Vibrations*, Van Dyke began to write lyrics to Brian's tunes for the next project, an album originally to be called *Dumb Angel.* (Whether or not there is any significance and connection in the fact that around this time Brian wrote and produced a single for Glen Campbell, entitled *Guess I'm Dumb,* is open to question.) Parks, had been a boy genius arranger and child actor in the '50s, and subsequently appeared in *The Swan* with Sir Alec Guiness and Grace Kelly and on records with such names as Little Feat, Arlo Guthrie, Randy Newman and Judy Collins.

Van Dyke later remembered: ''Brian sought me out, having heard about me from some mutual friends who later fell into disrepute with the Wilson clan because they were experimenting with psychedelics. At that time, people who experimented with psychedelics, no matter who they were, were viewed as enlightened people, and Brian sought out enlightened people.'' Which is not to say that Van Dyke was in any way responsible for turning Brian on to drugs — far from it. Apparently, Brian's conception of the *Dumb Angel* album was as a series of enquiries ''into the mind-expanding possibilities of music and the mind-expanding properties of drugs.''

The result was that the Wilson

house was frequently visited by eccentrics of all descriptions, which was not guaranteed to please the other Beach Boys, who were perhaps too 'respectable' to want to investigate the unknown. Despite the psychedelic revolution which would forever mark 1967 as the year of hippies, beads, love and peace and initial public experiments with psychedelic chemicals like LSD, the rest of the Beach Boys just weren't any part of the movement. As a result, they mostly left Brian alone to make the *Dumb Angel* album, the name of which at some point changed to *Smile,* suggested by a line in the song *Indian Wisdom* which says "The smile that you send out returns to you," which in itself was a fairly typical example of the kind of simplistic thinking pervading the times.

It appears that while the rest of the group were all for their music — as conceived by Brian — progressing, they felt that the finished tapes intended as *Smile* were unsuitable for a Beach Boys record, and could not be released as such. Mike Love: "I always appreciated the musical changes. The only thing that I didn't like about that period was that those guys hanging around Brian at that time were into a lot of drugs, and I didn't appreciate or dig that. And so I may have projected a bit of, if not animosity, then something

Lyricist Van Dyke Parks.

resembling it, towards people who would just come by and hang out with Brian and try to get him high and give him drugs."

Brian's version is somewhat different: "That *Dumb Angel,* we never finished it, because a lot of that shit just bothered me — but half of it we didn't finish anyway. Van Dyke Parks did a lot of it, and we used a lot of fuzz tone. It was inspiring, because Van Dyke is a very creative person, and it was a boost to me because he had a lot of energy and a lot of fresh ideas, so that energy has helped me. But a lot of the stuff was what I call little segments of songs, and it was a period when I was getting stoned and so we never really finished anything. We were into things that just didn't have any value for vocals, tracks that weren't made for vocals, so the group couldn't do it." Which is perhaps one reason why the rest of the group weren't keen to put their name to the record.

Whatever the truth, Brian was reported to have been so overwhelmed by the majority decision against him that he did not produce the group again — except to act as helper — until 1976.

There have been innumerable lists of tracks which were supposed to be part of the unreleased *Smile,* and some of them are recognizable as having

35

appeared on other, later albums. The obvious ones are *Surf's Up,* which was the title track of a much later LP, and had been performed once on television by just Brian at the piano on a Leonard Bernstein show where classics were mixed with pop music. In addition, there were *Heroes And Villains,* of which more later, and *Good Vibrations,* although this last predated the recording of the album. *Wind Chimes* and *Wonderful* were part of the *Smiley Smile* album which eventually replaced *Smile,* as was *Vegetables* (originally titled *Vega-Tables*). *Cabinessence* and *Our Prayer* appeared on the *20/20* album.

Which still leaves a bewildering array of tracks, about which little is known. *Old Master Painter, Grand Coulee Dam, You Are My Sunshine, Bicycle Rider, Can't Wait Too Long, Child Is Father To The Man, Do You Dig Worms, Barnyard* and *Holidays.* That's 17 tracks already, so perhaps Brian's 'segments' quote has a lot of truth in it. But it gets more complicated: *Cabinessence* was originally part of a longer song called *Who Ran The Iron Horse,* and was originally called *Home On The Range* — both alternative titles are part of the lyric to the eventually-released track. The *Iron Horse* title came from the song's subject matter — the building of the Transcontinental Railroad across America seen through the eyes of a Chinese coolie who was one of the construction gang.

The most celebrated part of *Smile* was the *Elements Suite,* a four-part epic devoted to an appreciation of the four elements of earth, air, fire and water. The water portion, apparently titled *I Love To Say Dada,* is allegedly a near-relation to *Cool, Cool Water.* This was a track which finally became part of the *Sunflower* album some time later, and is supposed to contain the original vocals from *Dada* on *Smile,* while *Good Vibrations,* the air portion, is obviously the same as the familiar version.

The other two parts of the suite are the most interesting. *Vegetables,* reasonably enough the earth section, is allegedly the nearest track to the original intended for *Smile* of any subsequently released. It is also supposed to have been a co-production between Brian Wilson and Paul McCartney, who was a great admirer of the Beach Boys in general and *Pet Sounds* in particular. Certainly there are witnesses to the fact that the Beatle was present at the sessions along with chief Byrd Roger McGuinn, and that a much longer version exists than that which came out on *Smiley Smile.* Others say that John Phillips, leader of the Mamas and Papas, was also on the session, playing percussion on bottles.

Brian was undoubtedly letting new experiences wash over him with

Capitol

alarming regularity, and at the same time was getting to know a lot of new people. McGuinn for example, was also involved in a bizarre American religious cult called Subud, which resulted in him changing his name from the original Jim to Roger, and Brian took a stab at that for a short time, as well as discovering numerology, the I Ching and doubtless other mystic 'wisdoms'. All that, and acid (LSD) as well!

But the clincher, and the reason most often given and accepted for the fact that *Smile* was a fragmented work is concerned with the fire section of the suite, entitled *Mrs O'Leary's Cow* after the beast which, tradition says, kicked over an oil lamp in its stall and started the Great Chicago Fire in 1871. Some years later, a Warner Brothers press release gave one version of the story: "During the recording of the album which was to have been released under the name *Smile,* Brian Wilson composed a piece of music known as *Mrs O'Leary's Cow,* but legendarily referred to as *Fire.* The music simulated fire itself, and was performed by leading Los Angeles studio musicians under the direction of Brian and Van Dyke Parks. Brian's wife, Marilyn, recalls rushing about Los Angeles purchasing firemen's hats for the musicians on the day of the session. The music is stimulating, and to some, frightening. A short time after the track was recorded, there

were, coincidentally, a number of major fires in the LA area. Whether they contributed to the year-long delay in the release of material intended for *Smile* or not, cannot be proven. The tapes of the recording session were never destroyed."

A journalist, Jules Siegel, who actually heard the track described it as follows: "A gigantic fire howled out of the massive studio speakers in a pounding crush of pictorial music that summoned up visions of roaring, wind-storm flames, falling timbers, mournful sirens and sweaty firemen, building up to a peak and crackling off into fading embers as a single drum turned into a collapsing wall and the fire engine cellos dissolved and disappeared." Shortly after Siegel was lucky enough to hear that, the building opposite the studio was destroyed by fire.

Frightened by the coincidence, Brian checked local fire statistics for that week which apparently showed there had been far more conflagrations than normal. Contrary to what the press release says, he is supposed to have destroyed the tapes of the track.

Carl Wilson, however, refuses to believe that, claiming that he'd subsequently heard the tapes, although he wasn't sure where they might be. Brian, talking in *Crawdaddy,* was adamant that he had got rid of everything. "It was destroying me — I was being destroyed thinking about it. It just wasn't my kind of music!" And of the *Fire* tracks being destroyed because he felt that the music had caused actual fires — "Yeah. And it made me think that [recording a song about fire] was a stupid thing to do, so I stopped. It scared me away."

On another occasion, this time talking to *Rolling Stone,* Brian's reaction was a little less direct. "We didn't finish it [*Smile*] because we had a lot of problems, inner group problems. We had time commitments we couldn't keep, so we stopped. Plus, for instance, we did a thing called the 'fire track'. We cut a song called *Fire* and we used fire helmets on the musicians and we put a bucket with fire burning in it in the studio so we could smell smoke while we cut. About a day later a building down the street burned down. We thought maybe it was witchcraft or something, we didn't know *what* we were into. So we decided not to finish it. Plus I got into drugs and I began doing things that were over my head. It was too fancy for the public. I got too fancy and arty and was doing things that were just not Beach Boys at all."

Talking to *Rolling Stone* on a different occasion Brian gave yet another version of the story. When asked why *Smile* had never been released, he said: "That was because . . . the lyrics, Van Dyke Parks had written lyrics that were all Van Dyke Parks and nothing of the Beach Boys. The lyrics were so poetic and symbolic, they were abstract, we couldn't . . . Oh no, wait, it was, no, really, I remember, this is it, this is why, it didn't come out because I'd bought a lot of hashish. It was really a large purchase, perhaps two thousand dollars-worth. We didn't realize, but the music was getting so influenced by it, the music had a really drugged feeling. I mean, we had to lie on the floor with the microphones next to our mouths to do the vocals. We didn't have any energy. I mean, you come into a session and see the group lying on the floor of the studio doing the vocals . . ."

The subject of this 'lost' Beach Boys album has provided endless conjecture making it impossible to separate truth from fiction. However, Brian has suggested in an interview that perhaps he really should start on the album where he left off, and finally realease it, fires or no fires. Of course, those of us eagerly waiting for that day could be extraordinarily disappointed.

Smile was intended to be the first album on the new Brother label owned by the Beach Boys which, of course, predated Apple. Brian had always wanted, in the now familiar cliché, to have an 'artist oriented record company', and a man had been hired to head it, David Anderle (later producer of the Ozark Mountain Daredevils). While Anderle was putting everything into motion from an administrative standpoint, a major complication occurred. Nick Grillo, the recently-appointed business manager (one of many who would try to serve the Beach Boys over the years) commenced a law suit claiming royalties of about a quarter of a million dollars alleged to be due to the group from Capitol, as a result of which law suits started to fly.

Brother Records & Independence

The law suit was eventually settled out of court, with Capitol paying some money to the group, and also agreeing to distribute the new label, but by then the idea was beginning to worry Brian. His initial concept had been not only to use Brother as an outlet for the Beach Boys and any other artists they might discover but also to release Brian Wilson albums of water noises, comedy and the fascinating 'health food album', although quite what this last might have entailed is anyone's guess. The only two signings to Brother ever authenticated were Danny Hutton, later a member of Three Dog Night, for whom it has been alleged that Brian was adapting *Good Vibrations,* and later *Darlin',* and a girl singer named Amy, said to resemble Mary Hopkin vocally. Nothing was released by either artist, or by Danny Hutton's group of the time, the Redwoods.

Apart from the 'artist orientation', one of the ideas behind Brother was perhaps to allow Brian to indulge his personal fantasies, on the basis that if he were allowed to do what he wanted, he might then additionally do some of the things that the rest of the group wanted; that is, help them to make commercial, accessible and successful records. But for various reasons, mostly connected with the law suit and hassles about setting up an independent operation, it suddenly didn't seem such a good idea.

In the '70s, Brother became a fairly well-established label, but its initial birth and death only amounted to a duration of a few months, with two releases, the single of *Heroes And Villains* and the eventual *Smiley Smile* album, during late summer of 1967. Inevitably, there had been a lot of anticipation concerning *Heroes And Villains* — early reports had suggested that it was "even better than *Good Vibrations,*" which was a somewhat presumptuous claim after the incredible success of that record, but the time between the two records was becoming ridiculously long. After six months, it was decided that a track from *Summer Days (And Summer Nights), Then I Kissed Her,* should be released in Britain, and it did well to reach number 4 in the chart, considering that it was a rather average remake of a Phil Spector-produced hit for the Crystals from five years before. In the States, Capitol issued *Best Of The Beach Boys Volume Two,* apparently allotting to it the same sort of promotional budget used for *Volume One,* which had annoyed Brian at the time as it was somewhat greater than that provided for *Pet Sounds.*

When *Heroes And Villains* was first released, because the agreement between Capitol and the Beach Boys by which the record company would distribute Brother releases had not been completed, it came out on Capitol, and was allegedly six and a half minutes long running through both sides of the single. Few people have heard that however, because soon afterwards the more familiar version came out on Brother in the States.

This was also the version which appeared in Britain, where it did slightly better than in America (it reached numbers 8 and 12 respectively). Capitol had obviously been trying to build anticipation for the single in the weeks before it was issued, and they must have been righteously indignant when only a few days before release date, Brian changed his mind about the record, and said he wanted to put out *Vegetables* instead. Fortunately for everyone concerned, he changed his mind yet again.

That wasn't the only touch of hysteria surrounding *Heroes And Villains,* as Terry Melcher recalled when talking to *Rolling Stone.* "Brian was holding onto this single, like 'All right, world — I've got it,' and waiting for the right time. He felt it was important to wait for the right time. This woman, I guess she was an astrologer — of sorts — came by Brian's house. She said to him 'Brian, the time is right,' and he was waiting for the word from this woman to release the record, I guess. He called the group. It was like 'OK, look. Here it is.' A small disc, seven inches. It was very solemn, very important, weighty. A heavy situation — it was all 'Brace yourself — for the big one.' All the group had limousines, and there was a caravan of Rolls Royces taking the record to KHJ [a very popular radio station in Los Angeles]. He was going to give the station an exclusive, just give it to them without telling Capitol.

"We got to the gates of KHJ, and the guard wouldn't let us in. A little talking, a little hubbub, a little bullshit, and the guard was finally intimidated enough by four or five Rolls Royce limousines to open his gate. We got in the building, got to the disc jockey who was presiding over the turntable. It was pretty late, probably around midnight. Brian said 'Hi, I'm Brian Wilson, here's the new Beach Boys single. I'd like to give you and KHJ an exclusive on it.' And this [guy] turned around and he said 'Can't play

Mass-celebrity transcendental meditation course in India. Left to right: Patti Boyd, John Lennon, Mike Love, the Maharishi, George Harrison, Mia Farrow, Donovan, Paul McCartney, Jane Asher and Cynthia Lennon. Right: tour publicity.

anything that's not on the playlist.' And Brian almost fainted. It was all over. He'd been holding the record, waiting for the right time, he'd had astrologers figuring out the correct moment. It really killed him. Finally, they played it, after a few calls to the program director or someone, who screamed 'Put it on, you idiot!' But the damage to Brian had already been done.''

38

After all that, and the comparative failure of the single (number 12 is a big comedown from *Good Vibrations'* number 1), not to mention the problems being experienced with Capitol and the formation of Brother, it's hardly surprising that *Smiley Smile,* when it was eventually released, was a bit of an anti-climax. Certainly, it's a very pleasant record, although hardly in the same league as *Pet Sounds,* despite the inclusion of obvious highlights like *Good Vibrations, Heroes And Villains* and *Vegetables.* The significant item is the production credit which is for the Beach Boys instead of Brian Wilson, and that's the way it was to stay for another nine years, until the release of *15 Big Ones.* Much of the record is supposed to have been re-

corded in an empty swimming pool, and the group have subsequently confessed that a certain amount of marijuana was in evidence. As a result of this, Dennis Wilson told *Rolling Stone* that he had at the time believed that Mike Love's song *She's Goin' Bald* was about oral sex.

It was to be the start of a long period of struggle for the Beach Boys, which wasn't helped in the public mind by the fact that they got involved with Maharishi Mahesh Yogi and 'Transcendental Meditation'. His introduction to the world of pop music was via George Harrison of the Beatles, who, it was said, was reacting extremely to the heavily drug-oriented society which was surrounding him. In the early part of 1967, Harrison went to

John Kelly

India to visit another of his idols, sitar player Ravi Shankar. Harrison became acquainted with the concept of meditation, and interested the other Beatles in this discipline, starting a bizarre landslide of showbiz personalities towards the art, including such famous names of this time as Donovan and Mia Farrow. Ringo Starr is quoted as saying "I've not taken any drugs since we started on this meditation. I hope I'll get so much out of this that I won't have to go back on drugs." Suddenly, it was very fashionable to meditate although it's to the Beach Boys' credit that they didn't become involved until after the initial wave of hysteria had passed.

The first member of the group to meet the Maharishi was Dennis Wilson. The Beach Boys were in Europe, and among their engagements was a benefit concert in Paris for UNICEF, in December, 1967. Dennis had left the rest of the group in London, and was watching Ravi Shankar rehearse for the show, when he spotted the Maharishi in the audience. "I shook his hand, and all of a sudden I felt this weirdness, this presence, the guy had," Dennis told *New Times.* "'Live your life to the fullest' was the first thing he ever said to me. So the next day I went over to his room, and he said 'Tell me some words of your songs.' I told him the lyrics to *God Only Knows,* and he goes 'That's the sun rising, and the stars and the planets, and it connects with . . .' I thought it was great, and he said 'We'd like to initiate you into the program.' I said 'What does that mean? How much?' and he said 'We'll just do it to you tomorrow morning.' So I called Michael and all the guys in London, 'C'mon down here in Paris, we're all gonna meditate.' And then I got my mantra [a word or phrase to be constantly repeated during meditation], and as Maharishi was giving them to us he says 'What do you want?', and I said 'I want everything, everything.' And he laughed, and we meditated together. It was so wild."

Dennis Wilson was the most unlikely Beach Boy to introduce the group to meditation, but in many ways it was an act of fate that they became involved, for in the years to come, they were certainly going to need some sort of mental prop.

39

Crisis, Change & Chaos
1968-70

Just about the same time as the rest of the Beach Boys were meeting the Maharishi for the first time, having left Brian Wilson at home in Los Angeles, the next LP after the failure of *Smiley Smile* was being released. Capitol, with whom the group had fought ever since the release of *Pet Sounds* 18 months before, had been making sure that there were plenty of Beach Boys records on the market, and released a three album repackage of *Beach Boys Today, Summer Days (And Summer Nights)* and *Pet Sounds* under the joint name of *Beach Boys Deluxe Set*. The group disapproved of the package and this move helped bring forward the day when the Beach Boys would finally leave the company.

Manson & Maharishi

But that problem was a minor one compared with what would be Dennis Wilson's major hassle of 1968, and one which even years later he refused to discuss. "No. Never. As long as I live I'll never talk about that. I don't know anything, you know? If I did, I would've been up on that witness stand" was his answer to a question on the subject of Charles Manson addressed to him by *Rolling Stone* in 1976. And there's little doubt that anyone else who had been involved with a convicted murderer would have felt equally reticent.

Dennis first met Manson and his murderous band in the first half of the year, either as a result of being picked up while hitch-hiking by a member of 'The Family', as Manson's crew were known, or because he picked up a hitcher himself — Ella Sinder, another member of the pack, who is supposed to have resembled Greta Garbo. The latter version sounds closer to the truth, but whoever it was who did the introductions, soon Dennis became a close associate of The Family, and in particular of Manson, who had ambitions to be a rock star. It wasn't long before a large number of Family members had entrenched themselves in Dennis's house, a three acre site on Sunset Boulevard near the ocean in Pacific Palisades.

Manson also ingratiated himself with Terry Melcher, who had successfully produced the Byrds and Paul Revere and the Raiders, among several others. Melcher, of course, had also worked extensively during the early and mid-'60s with Bruce Johnston, so he was another influential connection for Manson in his quest for stardom. Just to complete Manson's trio of useful people, he also cultivated one Gregg Jakobson, who was a friend and employee of Melcher, and at some point shared a house with Dennis Wilson.

Dennis was fascinated by Manson.

He seemed to have a magnetic power which drew disciples around him. He expounded his bizarre and often sacrilegious philosophies to them, and they appear to have supported him financially for long periods. For some time, the Wilson residence was crowded with Manson's people — one was even employed by him as a gardener for a while — using the facilities Dennis put at their disposal. It got to the point where Manson used Dennis's address both to impress his parole officer and also on his identity card, and not long after, Dennis took several of his 'guests' to a Beach Boys gig in Colorado.

Around this time, on a British tour with the Beach Boys, Dennis Wilson uttered one of his most reprinted quotes during an interview with *Rave* magazine. "Fear is nothing but awareness. I was only frightened as a child because I didn't understand fear; it all came from within. Sometimes 'The Wizard' frightens me. 'The Wizard' is Charles Manson, who is another friend of mine, who says he is God and the Devil. He sings, plays and writes poetry, and may be another artist on Brother Records." It's possible that Dennis's association with the evil Manson was some kind of reaction to everyone else's involvement with the Maharishi. He had been the first member of the group to meet the guru, so perhaps he wanted to continue being ahead of his brothers and cousin.

Of course, it didn't quite work out that way. Although the Maharishi obviously welcomed the publicity involved in numbering pop stars among his followers, there was no question of his ripping off any saleable property belonging to the Beach Boys. Manson, on the other hand, wanted the material stuff as well as the fame, and The Family reduced Dennis's wealth considerably during their stay.

In the summer of 1968, Manson even got inside Brian Wilson's studio, where he recorded several songs, ostensibly for a forthcoming album on Brother. According to Ed Sanders' book *The Family*, from which much of this information was gleaned, Manson wrote a song that day in an effort to encourage the various Beach Boys to stop quarreling among themselves. The title of that song was *Cease To Exist*, which the group changed to *Cease To Resist*, and finally recorded it — with no participation from Manson — under the title *Never Learn Not To Love*, the B-side of *Bluebirds Over The Mountain*, which was released late in 1968. The reason why Manson's name fails to appear on the record as composer was explained by Dennis thus: "He didn't want a label credit, he wanted money instead. I gave him about $100,000 worth of stuff."

That, of course, was a retrospective quote, because at the time, there's no

doubt that Dennis, Melcher and Gregg Jakobson were besotted with Manson. Wilson and Melcher even tried to persuade a successful manager named Rudy Altobelli to handle him. Fortunately, the infatuation didn't last too long, and the final straw is supposed to have been Dennis's discovery that The Family, apart from wearing and giving away all his clothes, had done likewise with his impressive collection of gold Beach Boys records. Dennis thereupon decided to move out, allowing the other residents to remain for a while, before he got his manager to evict them, by which time there was little of value left in the house. In the meantime, a 16-year-old Mansonite had destroyed Dennis's expensive red Ferrari, and Manson had visited Dennis Wilson and Gregg Jakobson in an unsuccessful attempt to get them to become full time members of The Family.

Until the single with his song *Never Learn Not To Love* on it was released, Manson felt it necessary to maintain a friendly relationship with Dennis, even if the latter seemed to be one of the few people in his immediate circle who wouldn't accede to the Manson command. When it did come out, and failed to make the Top 20, Manson blamed the lack of success on the change of words, although the song was quite definitely his — it even contained a Manson "relaxation mantra" which was added to the final part of the record.

Somewhat later, another Manson follower, Bobby Beausoleil, also contacted Dennis with a view to getting his songs recorded, and at a later Manson recording session in 1969, sang backing vocals watched by Dennis, Terry Melcher and Gregg Jakobson. But despite the growing suspicion which was beginning to surround Manson, his music business pals were still trying to help him into the big time. Gregg Jakobson, in particular, wanted Terry Melcher to make a documentary TV film to form part of his mother's *Doris Day Show*, showing The Family at work and play, and with Manson singing, but Charlie refused to sign the necessary contracts, most fortunately for everyone involved.

It didn't stop there — Manson contacted his parole officer in 1969 asking permission to be absent from Los Angeles for a while, because he had been booked (for $5,000, or so he said) as the support act on a Beach Boys tour of Texas. That never came off (if, indeed, it had ever been a possibility in the first place) because the parole officer insisted on some kind of documentary proof, like a letter from the Beach Boys' management. After that, things became a little quieter for Dennis, although after Manson committed several of his celebrated murders, he twice asked Dennis

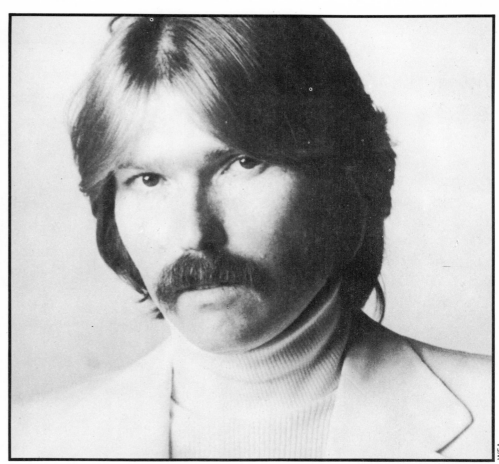

Left: Charles Manson. Right: Terry Melcher, singer/songwriter who produced the Byrds and the Raiders.

for loans, and when he was turned down, threatened to kill Scotty Wilson, Dennis's son by his first marriage. That was almost the end of the nightmare for Dennis, but for Terry Melcher, worse was to come.

Terry had aroused Manson's ire by asking him to sign contracts, and in terms of self-preservation, arousing Charlie's ire was not recommended. First off, The Family stole a telescope from Melcher's home which was set up outside his beach house. He could put up with that. But it was when the Manson gang slaughtered everyone at a house in which Melcher used to live — and had not long vacated — that he must have started to wonder whether it was not Sharon Tate, the film star and wife of movie director Roman Polanski, whom Manson was after, but himself. Even after a number of Manson followers were imprisoned for murder and/or conspiracy to commit murder, there were still quite a number at liberty on the streets who might have sought revenge for the imprisonment of their leader, and to continue the bestiality he had started. Apparently, there was a 'death list' prepared by Manson of those whom he felt deserved to be killed, most of them owing their inclusion to the fact that they had in some way crossed Manson by not agreeing to one or other of his ludicrous proposals. It's quite possible that Terry Melcher was on the list, and there's a very good

chance that it may also have included Dennis Wilson and Gregg Jakobson. (Incidentally, the two continued their association; Jakobson produced Dennis's first solo LP.)

Bruce Johnston, when asked whether the Manson gang had killed the wrong people on that horrific night at Melcher's ex-home when Sharon Tate and others were slaughtered was categoric that they made no mistake. "Manson knew where Terry lived, because he'd been there. Terry didn't find out about some of this until later, and he worried about it, of course, but he discovered that he wasn't the intended victim. Manson used to come up to Brian's house a lot, and Brian probably had a lot of tapes of Manson, although I never sang on any of the sessions. But I did go over to Dennis's house and talk to Manson — he had a lot of 1968 psychedelic charisma. As far as Terry's connection with Manson goes, he was just a music publisher who turned Manson's songs down, and there's a track about it on Terry's first album. If you listen to the words, you'll kind of understand it more." The song was *Halls Of Justice* and the words may throw light on the subject.

Seemed like a simple audition, there were just a few songs getting sung.
I had no way of knowing, but it was me about to get hung.
It seemed like another audition, people

singing songs of brotherly love.
I just can't imagine what they must have been thinking, I never dreamed what they were thinking of.

The rest of the Beach Boy clan weren't too pleased with Dennis's criminal connections, especially when the *Los Angeles Times* front-paged the story. Audree Wilson, Dennis' mother recounted the events to *Rolling Stone* in 1976. "I was absolutely horrified, terrified. First of all, when Manson and his family, the girls, moved in with Dennis. Dennis had this beautiful place at Will Rogers State Park, right off Sunset, and he befriended them. They were just hippies and he thought Manson was the nicest person, a very gentle, nice guy. Murry had a fit, because he knew there were a bunch of girls living there. I went there one day. Dennis was at the recording studio in Brian's house, and he asked me if I'd take him home. I was very hesitant because I thought Murry wouldn't like it, but I took him home, and he said 'Will you just come in and meet them? Come on, they're nice.' So I went in, and Charlie Manson was walking through this big yard with a long robe on, and Dennis introduced me.

"I just thought he looked older than he supposedly is, like an older man, and I thought he had a kind face. That was the only impression I had. And I did think they were a bunch of

leeches; Dennis had been through that before. He could never stand to see anyone who needed anything or anybody who had any kind of problem — he was right there. Then when that horrible story came out about Manson's arrest for the Sharon Tate murder, Annie, Carl's wife called me. I didn't connect at all that that was the same person and the same family who had been with Dennis. When she told me, I just totally froze. When they left Dennis's house, Manson or somebody stole Dennis's Ferrari, and they stole everything in the house that could be moved. Everything. Stripped. Dennis had kicked them out because they were into heavy drugs, and he just wanted them out.''

In an earlier *Rolling Stone* interview, an anonymous Beach Boy (for obvious reasons) was more critical. ''Charlie struck me as a very intense and dogmatic type. I didn't want anything to do with him. He was living with Dennis at the time, when Dennis was just divorced — I suppose the life style appealed to him. Perhaps I have more sexual inhibitions, moral strictures, but I wasn't into drugs at that point, which was Charlie's way of conditioning his little friends, turning them into egoless entities. I wasn't going for his pitch. Dennis ran up the largest gonorrhea bill in history the time the whole family got the clap. He took them all to a Beverly Hills doctor — it took something like a thousand dollars in penicillin.''

While all this was going on, the Beach Boys were continuing their feud with Capitol Records. The next album released, in December 1967, was *Wild Honey*, generally accepted as an unexceptional record by Beach Boys standards. It was preceded by the title track in single form (with a *Smiley Smile* track, *Wind Chimes*, on the B-side) but it wasn't a great success, being the first single by the group not to reach the Top 20 for some considerable time. One reason for the decline in the group's popularity was the burgeoning San Francisco sound of the late '60s — bands like the Grateful Dead, the Jefferson Airplane, Quicksilver Messenger Ser-

44

Capitol

The boys with Murry Wilson — their first manager and mentor.

psychedelic in '67 or '68, with flower power, lover of the beach . . .'' Even if that's what Mike feels now, there's little doubt that even when he originally said it, a lead singer with so little hair could hardly qualify as a boy!

The *Wild Honey* album, despite the fact that it's still far from a classic, has gleaned a certain amount of retrospective acclaim, perhaps because some of the Beach Boys' records which it preceded were considerably inferior. It was the first album recorded in the newly-installed studio in Brian's house in Bel Air, but Brian had less to do with the production than ever before; he was starting to hand that responsibility over to Carl. ''When we did *Wild Honey*, Brian asked me to get more involved in the recording end. He wanted a break. He was tired. He had been doing it all too long.''

Critics have likened *Wild Honey* to Bob Dylan's *John Wesley Harding*, which it preceded, in that both demonstrated a strong reversion to simplicity and to some extent turned their backs on technology. It also confirmed, perhaps for the first time, Murry's insistence that Brian was able to contribute strongly to black music and be influenced by it. The confirmation is in the R&B slant of the music on the album — although there's only one song which is obviously from a non-white field, Stevie Wonder's *I Was Made To Love Her*, many of the others without doubt take a different inspiration from what had gone before. Nick Kent in *New Musical Express* reckoned that Brian had done a good deal of listening to the products of Tamla Motown, but Bruce Johnston explained the change as a simple reversion to less complicated music, inspired by the fact that most of them admired some aspects of black music.

In the same piece, Carl Wilson filled out that explanation: ''*Wild Honey* was very simply music to cool out by. Brian was still very spaced out, though I seem to recall he'd given up acid by that time. His thing with acid was short, but very intense, plus we, the whole band, were smoking this really heavy dope. That's why *Smiley Smile* sounds the way it does. But we all really dug Motown, so Brian reckoned we should get more into a white R&B bag. I also recall around that time the band, and Brian in particular, getting criticized very heavily for sounding like choir boys.''

Whatever the reasons, while critics of the era remained unimpressed, the album did provide a reasonable-sized hit single in *Darlin'*, which charted both in Britain and America, and was enough the keep the group close to the public's view of where it was at. *Darlin'*, you'll recall, had originally been meant for the Redwoods, who

were signed to Brother during that abortive period just before *Smile*. If the Redwoods project had come to fruition, perhaps one of the world's most consistent chart-making groups would never have been formed. Danny Hutton's next group after the Redwoods, Three Dog Night, specialized in covering songs by a variety of writers, including Randy Newman, Leo Sayer, Hoyt Axton, Russ Ballard and many more, reducing them all to middle of the road rock.

Mike Love looked back ruefully: ''There was one of the stupidest mistakes in the world of recording. Three Dog Night sold more single records than anybody in the world, and Brian Wilson produced them originally, but, you know, it was funny. They'd go in [as the Redwoods] and they wouldn't sing well enough for him. He didn't want to hear any sharps or flats. He was at that period of his life where he was horrible to live with. But he's great musically — that's why our music has lasted, because he was such a stickler for perfection, and he would hear them sharp or flat, or they didn't have the quality. It's not just the note being sung, it's the particular pitch and timbre, and subtle overt and covert implications that Brian's looking for. Who knows, cosmic or whatever, but the fact of the matter is that he had them in the studio for several days, and he was really funny. They didn't meet up to his expectations, but they went off and made billions.''

While Dennis was involved with Charles Manson, Carl Wilson and Mike Love were also involved in enterprises external to the group, and even Brian indulged another of his whims, opening a health food shop called The Radiant Radish situated in West Hollywood, where he occasionally served behind the counter.

Meanwhile, Carl was joining a growing number of his generation in resisting the draft notice which had told him that Uncle Sam desperately needed him to fight communism in Vietnam. Carl, reasonably enough, claimed that he was a conscientious objector, but the army turned that down, so Carl refused to attend his induction course. At that point, he was allowed officially to call himself a conscientious objector, and was thus sent to work as an orderly in a hospital. He again refused, saying that he would do anything at all that the government required, using his trade as a musician. It's suggested that Carl offered to play benefit concerts which would feature the Beach Boys, but that didn't seem to happen, although since that time, there's no doubt at all that the group have supported several causes they deem worthy.

Mike Love was the Beach Boy who really got involved in the Maharishi and Transcendental Meditation, which

vice and the like were turning a great many record buyers' heads and to be last year's thing was tantamount to ceasing to exist.

Around this time, Mike Love said in an interview that he thought it might not be such a bad idea to streamline the group's name, perhaps to simply 'Beach', but more recently he has indicated that the suggestion wasn't to be taken too seriously. ''That was a statement that I rather facetiously uttered in jest with some dry and caustic humor, when once upon a time I was asked if we had ever thought of changing our name, and I said 'Well, we've thought about dropping the Boys' — to call ourselves the Beach would be very hip and

Capitol

we shall hereafter refer to as TM. A few months after he first met up with the Maharishi in Paris, Mike went to India to study TM, and as a result, both he and Al Jardine became teachers of the discipline. Mike: "The whole group meditates — any group is only as strong as its members, and I don't think I'd be in the group if it wasn't for meditation. It raises your tolerance to stress, it helps against the fatiguing effects of physical and mental activity." Carl Wilson, although less formally involved than his cousin, agrees: "I meditate regularly. It's helped me to cope with things, things affect me less. Bad things, or rather difficult things, affect me less. I find that it relaxes me very deeply and gives me energy. I recommend it highly."

There's one thing that the Maharishi is alleged to have said which, if it's true, might be thought extremely impressive. The story goes that he once prophesied that if the Beatles continued to meditate, they would stay together, and if the Beach Boys meditated, they would become the most influential group in the world. We know what happened in both cases, of course, although it's difficult to prove that non-meditation was the key factor among the many which resulted in the passing of the Beatles.

Despite the fact that even now most of the Beach Boys acknowledge the Maharishi as an influence on their lives, during the early stages of their relationship a near-disaster occurred, and the fact that all the parties have lived through it with their alliance unaffected says much for TM. Mike Love, fired with enthusiasm for the Maharishi and his unimpeachable desire for world peace, persuaded the rest of the group to embark upon what was planned as a worldwide tour to 'introduce' the guru to countries and people unaware of him. Some commentators have decided that the move was made too early, before the idea of TM was acceptable to more than a small aware élite, but whatever the reason, the tour was considerably less than an unqualified success. Love even went to Europe, where he hoped to organize concerts under the general heading of 'World Peace 1', with a projected 'World Peace 2' taking in Moscow and Bangkok.

Love told *New Musical Express:* "We are hoping to involve as many creative people in all forms of art and entertainment, as possible, from Picasso to Hefner's bunny girls. Some of the most famous names in the pop world have guaranteed their assistance." Later in the same interview, Love, "fired with earnest conviction," said "Did you know that the Maharishi met the UN Secretary General U Thant in America, and Thant said that the Maharishi made more sense in 15 minutes than he had heard in 30 years!"

Unfortunately, the first leg of the world tour, across America, was an unmitigated disaster. Apparently, the tour was booked into huge halls, in the expectation that a large audience would come to see either this new peacemaker or the Beach Boys, or both, but a sad miscalculation had been made. Very few people at that time were interested in meditation, and the Beach Boys were not exactly at the peak of their popularity. Audiences wanted to hear the old hits from the early part of the '60s, not the complex music initiated with *Pet Sounds,* and they stayed away in droves. Even the few that did bother to go to the concerts were vociferous in their disapproval of the 'performance', and after only two concerts, even Mike Love was apparently forced to admit that his master plan just wasn't going to bear fruit.

Bruce Johnston, talking to *New Musical Express* later that year (1968) was philosophical about it. "I think that everyone should do a tour like that and have the experience of losing three or four hundred thousand dollars — it's real funky! Now we're spending all our time making up the money we lost. But Mike didn't lose faith in the Maharishi and he still meditates. None of us have lost faith in the method." And that comes from the Beach Boy generally accepted as being the one least concerned with meditation.

Subsequently, it's been claimed that there may be a correlation between the increasing popularity of TM and the similar ascendancy of the Beach Boys star — who can say whether that's a possibility? Certainly, though, the group had to put on permanent display their enthusiasm for the movement, and strong TM influences were evident in their new LP, *Friends.* Although *Friends* was scheduled as the next new album, the almost inevitable happened, and Capitol put out something else. The 'something else' in this case was an album which, until the mid-'70s had been one of the most sought-after Beach Boys records, although the group would no doubt wish to disown it. *Stack O'Tracks* is a 15-cut LP consisting purely of the backing tracks to some well-known Beach Boy songs, without any vocals at all. The theory is that vocals are provided by the listener(s), and to this end, the original American version of the record came with a full musical score including the words. The record wasn't issued in Britain until 1976 and instead of a musical score, just the words were added to the package. It's a curio — devout Beach Boys fans will usually defend the record to the death, but it was a rather strange offering from a group who have often admitted that their vocals were the strength of their appeal.

First time out in America, it wasn't too successful, which in many ways is a blessing, because had it sold even respectably, no doubt it would have been followed by another half dozen volumes using the identical recipe. By the time it came out in Britain for the first time, some eight years after the American release, it had become a bona fide collector's item, and it is rumored that significant quantities of the British pressing were exported to America. One noteworthy point about *Stack. O'Tracks* was made by a writer in *New Musical Express* in 1973. ". . . it offers interesting insight into how BB songs are constructed. Were you aware nearly all the melody lines are supplied by voices?"

Sadly, *Friends* failed to produce a hit single. The group were getting somewhat erratic in their chart stabs, and since *Heroes And Villains* there had been one hit (*Darlin'*) and two flops (*Gettin' Hungry,* a *Smiley Smile* track, and *Wild Honey*). The title track of *Friends* wasn't any help when it hit the streets, and in many ways the album was equally lacking in hit quality. However, one thing it did succeed in doing was bringing to the fore the writing talents of the rest of the group, replacing Brian's previous dominance. Strangely, the most prolific initially was Dennis Wilson, perhaps on the rebound from his recent divorce, and not yet fully aware of the impact Charles Manson, whom he had just met, would have on his life. Dennis was involved in no less than five of

the 12 tracks on the album, and Al Jardine in a similar number, although in a more supportive role.

Friends was also the first Beach Boys album to be recorded in genuine stereo, as by now Carl, without a hearing affliction, was taking a major part in production duties. It is reportedly Brian Wilson's favorite Beach Boy album, which even surprises the other members of the group. "Yeah, it's weird. Brian really has a thing about that album. He really loves it." However, there is one particular track on *Friends* which most critics seem to find fascinating, a song totally written by Brian, on which he sings solo in front of a gentle bossa nova backing, sounding rather like Chris Montez on *The More I See You.* The song is called *Busy Doin' Nothin',* and that's more or less what it's about, with vague directions as to how to reach Brian's house (where he can be found doing nothing), and a lyric which is full to the brim of mundane occurrences, such as telephoning someone and discovering that they're not in. The rest of the album isn't any more weighty — the return to basics of *Wild Honey* was continued, but this time combined with the TM idea, and almost inevitably, one of the tracks is entitled *Transcendental Meditation.* While most members of the group had personal problems there's not much doubt that the period between the release of *Friends* and the group's final break from Capitol Records was one of the lowest points in the Beach Boys' history.

By this time, Capitol had released five non-original albums since *Pet Sounds* and only three new LPs. Apart from *Stack O'Tracks* and the three album *Deluxe Set,* the *Best Of* series was up to Volume Three, although the tracks selected were still predominantly taken from the pre-*Pet Sounds* era. That certainly didn't help, anymore than the group's reaction, which was to tour America a little later with a repertoire which purposely excluded all material from before *Pet Sounds.* This succeeded in alienating a large portion of their potential audience, in addition to the large number who had indicated their impatience with the group by failing to support the tour with the Maharishi. And then there was the Jimi Hendrix quote. Sometime in 1968, after setting the world alight with four hit singles in Britain within eight months, Hendrix proclaimed to the listening rock audience "Now we'll never have to listen to surf music again." Although the remark was probably not made maliciously or with any intention of upsetting the Beach Boys, it did make an impression on the Beach Boys' remaining fans.

As if all this wasn't enough, Murry Wilson, for some time a silent observer of the group he had helped to conceive, suddenly demonstrated his lack

of faith in what was going on by selling his rights to all the Beach Boys material to A&M Records' music publishing arm. According to Nick Kent in *New Musical Express,* the purchase was made without too much forethought, and subsequently Tony Asher, a previous collaborator of Brian's, was asked by A&M if he'd be interested in writing fresh lyrics to some of the songs. It is a tribute to Asher that he refused.

But the real problem was with Capitol Records, as Mike Love explained: ". . . we got a contract with Capitol Records . . . and we were living under that . . . specter (and I don't mean Phil) for about eight or nine years until we finally got out of it . . . They promoted us very well for the first four or five years, then they failed . . . in promoting the change, which would have been very commercially sensible on their part, but they didn't ever do it. In '68 or '69, they were still promoting us as the number one surfing group in the USA. How relevant was that after *Good Vibrations, Pet Sounds, Smiley Smile* or Vietnam and everything else?"

What it all amounted to was that the group were blaming their record company for their lack of success, and the record company were blaming the group for changing their style. It was obvious that something would have to give, but before that could happen, the group had to honor their contract by making two more albums for Capitol before they were free to go. One of these was *20/20,* an album which on the face of it looks quite good, spawning four singles, three of which were hits. But in actuality, *20/20* is a rag bag of old tracks, mostly out-takes from earlier albums. For example, two of the *Smile* tracks, *Cabinessence* and *Our Prayer* finally made their public appearance, and a couple of *Friends* out-takes, *I Want To Sleep* and *Time To Get Alone,* are also included. As far as the hits go, *Do It Again, I Can Hear Music* and *Cottonfields* all did well in Britain. *Do It Again* made number 1 and was the only one of the three to penetrate the American Top 20, and then only in 20th position.

Each of the three tracks has something recorded about it by one or other of the group. Bruce Johnston, visiting London in September 1968, agreed with a reporter who said he didn't think much of *Do It Again.* "I don't like it either. I don't think that the group were entirely happy with it, but everyone else was going back to basics, so I suppose it was inevitable that we should." Then in *Who Put The Bomp,* Brian Wilson, talking about his admiration for Phil Spector, said "One of my favorite Beach Boys records is *I Can Hear Music,* which was by the Ronettes originally. That was Carl singing lead on that, and as a matter of fact he produced it too." As far as

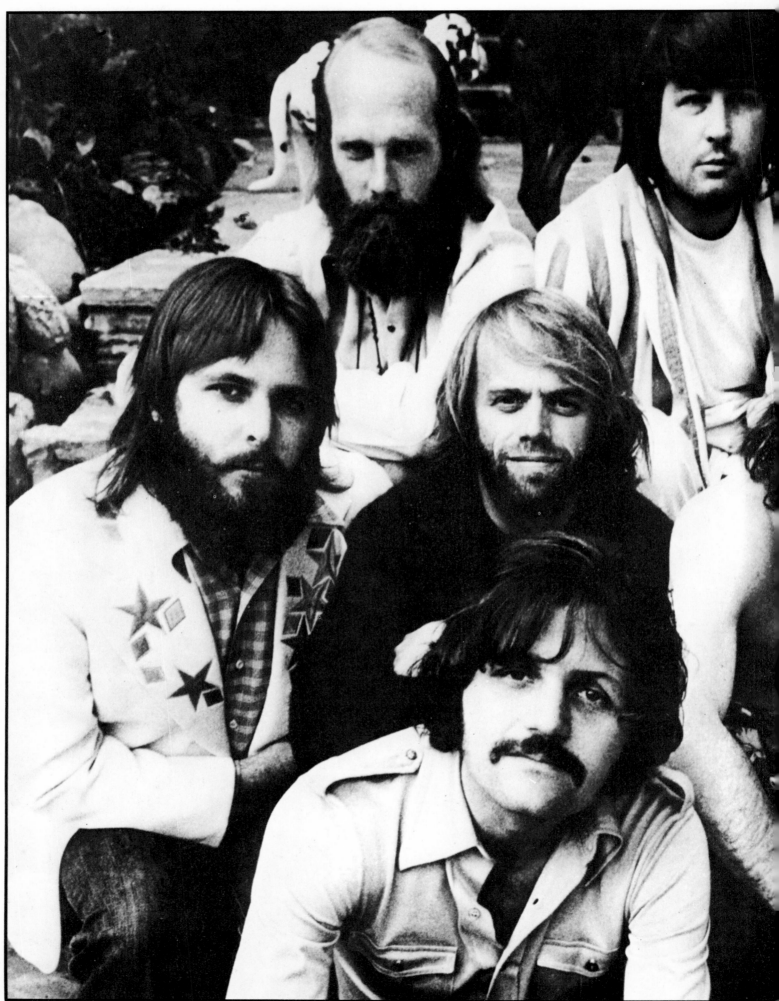

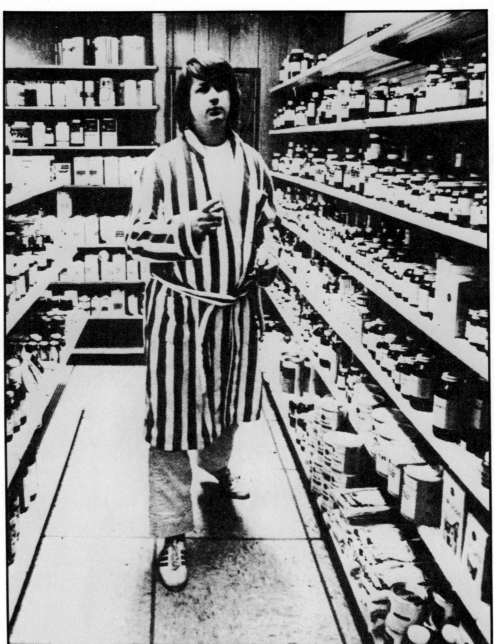

Brian Wilson in his Los Angeles health-food store, The Radiant Radish.

Cottonfields goes, several members of the group have attributed the idea behind the record to Al Jardine's folk background, in much the same way that the inspiration behind *Sloop John B* was owed to Al. In fact, the group liked the song so much that they also put it on their next album.

20/20 also included a single which failed, *Bluebirds Over The Mountain,* a song written by Ersel Hickey which had previously been a single for Richie Valens, who died in the same airplane as Buddy Holly. The B-side of the Beach Boys *Bluebirds* was, of course, *Never Learn Not To Love,* which gave Charles Manson his brief flirtation with the music business. A further innovation was noted on the album's sleeve which listed production credits. This is quite illuminating because it was the first time since Brian dropped the reins that individual

credits were given. Brian, of course, produced the earlier tracks, but the group was now sufficiently democratic to give each of the other five some kind of production credit.

20/20 came close to fulfilling the Capitol contract, but another album was still required. At one point, that was going to be an album called *The Fading Rock Group Revival,* a sarcastic title indeed, but that was eventually shelved, and many of the tracks appeared on the group's next studio album. To complete the contract, the group decided on another live album, which was actually made even before the release of *20/20,* while the group were touring Britain.

On December 1, 1968, the Beach Boys made their final album for Capitol — *Live In London* — at the London Palladium. The selection of songs is quite interesting, in that nine of the 12

53

are fairly well known, the least familiar being *Bluebirds Over The Mountain,* at that time the current single, while the *Wild Honey* and *Friends* albums each have one of their more obscure songs performed live, and there's one track, *Their Hearts Were Full Of Spring,* a song written by Bobby Troup, better known for composing *Route 66,* that had only previously appeared on *Little Deuce Coupe* as *A Young Man's Gone.* The melody was the same but the lyrics were different, being a tribute to the late James Dean. The album was released in England in 1970, but didn't come out in America until 1977, providing some kind of reversed parallel with *Stack O'Tracks.* Other than a one-off single, *Break Away,* that was the last recording the Beach Boys made for Capitol, having fulfilled their contract. Finally they were free from what they considered to be a constraining contract and they could start trying to re-shape their career, which was undoubtedly in tatters.

While it seems laughable now that the Beach Boys might have difficulty getting a new record deal, there's some doubt as to just how easy it was for them to come to an agreement with Warner/Reprise Records. Fortunately,

the chairman of that company, Mo Ostin, had a healthy respect for the group, believing them to be, in Van Dyke Parks' words "a crucial, highly-appealing slice of Americana which was simply unique, and should never be dismissed or ignored out of hand."

The new deal also meant that the Brother label could restart after its abortive beginnings around *Smile* time, and the first release on Brother/Reprise was *Sunflower,* which was to mark the end of one era, and the beginning of another. A further stipulation of the move to Reprise was that the Beach Boys albums since 1966 should also be licensed to the incoming company by Capitol, and as they were the least successful items in their catalog, Capitol weren't too worried about agreeing, although that particular deal didn't take in the British market, where Capitol retained the rights.

By the time *Sunflower* came out in the spring of 1970, another Beach Boys curio had been created. In a move so far unexplained, Dennis Wilson made a single for the Stateside label, which was apparently only released in Britain. The titles of this exceedingly rare article were *Sound Of Free* and *Lady,* which were credited to 'Dennis

Wilson and Rumbo'. No-one seems to have ever asked Dennis what the idea was behind this burst of independence, but it's possible that there's some connection with the fact that *Sunflower,* and in fact *Surf's Up,* the next two Beach Boys albums, were released in Britain on the Stateside label.

Sunflower, despite being the first product of the new company, didn't differ too much from its immediate predecessor, although it appears in retrospect to have attracted rather more critical acclaim than it deserves. Bruce Johnston, talking some time after he'd left the group in *New Musical Express,* felt that it was a very significant album for the group. "*Sunflower* is the last real Beach Boys album, simply because it's the last album Brian personally directed — the last album which recognized the need for a monarchial figure to be up there calling the shots as opposed to the pussyfooting democracy which ended up splitting all their subsequent albums up into sections." In fairness, it should be noted that Bruce wasn't going to be in the group for too long after *Sunflower* . . . Other critics felt that the record marked the start of the performing Beach Boys as a solid unit,

for the first time getting away from Brian's overall control, so it's very difficult to judge just how important the album really is.

In terms of the material, it's spread fairly evenly around the various group members, although Carl lags behind the rest. Dennis again was prolific, at this point nearing the end of his Manson traumas, and Bruce came out with one of the more clear-cut successes of the album in *Tears In The Morning*, a worthy predecessor to his later writing triumphs. The first single from *Sunflower* was *Add Some Music To Your Day*, which was rumored to be the album's original title, and there's yet another excerpt from *Smile* in *Cool, Cool Water* from the *Elements Suite*. On British versions of the record, there's a bonus track, an alternative take of *Cottonfields*, although why this should have happened is not at all clear. In terms of hit singles, the album was a wash-out, coming out at a time when the group were still at a very low ebb of popularity. Something really had to be done about the lost credibility of the Beach Boys . . .

Three things happened. First off, Brian briefly returned to live performance, coming on stage with the group at the Whiskey-A-Go-Go in Los Angeles, which in fact was the first 'local' gig the group had played in three years. Unfortunately, the fairy tale aspects of Big Brother's return were dissipated when his bad ear began to trouble him again, and he abandoned live work for another long period. Secondly, the Beach Boys played at the Second Monterey Festival at Big Sur, a move calculated to win the favor of the 'alternative society', as among the other artists appearing were Country Joe McDonald, Joan Baez, Linda Ronstadt and Kris Kristofferson, fresh from being beer-canned off the stage at the final Isle of Wight Festival, where nobody had heard of him.

For the Beach Boys to play Monterey was a good move from several other aspects. The proceeds of the Festival went to the 'Institute For The Study Of Non-Violence', which brought the group into the vision of the growing anti-Vietnam peace movement. Then there was the point that the group had been supposed to perform at the first Monterey Festival, in 1967, when Brian Wilson was on the board of organizers, but had eventually decided to give it a miss because the concept of the Festival had altered so many time. That didn't go down well with the hip élite of Hollywood. The 1970 Festival was a shrewd move for the Beach Boys by way of making amends and they even appeared on the resultant album, *Celebration,* which came out on A&M. They only had one track on the album while all the others on the record had two, but it was undoubtedly a successful gesture to allow *Wouldn't It Be Nice* to appear on another label. The credibility gap was gradually being closed, and even *Rolling Stone* magazine, who had not long before vented some spleen on the Beach Boys, admitted that they had played very well.

At about this time Brian met a man who was to prove very significant to the Beach Boys over the next few years. While serving in his health food shop, The Radiant Radish, he struck up a friendship with a customer named Jack Rieley. Rieley was originally a disc jockey at an LA radio station, who interviewed the group on the air, and got on so well with Mike Love and Brian that he was invited to Brian's house. He was soon a trusted confidant of the Beach Boys, and figured largely in the next stage of their career.

Surf's Down
1971-74

WEA

When Jack Rieley first met Brian Wilson on a visit to The Radiant Radish in 1970, he was already a long time Beach Boys fan and immediately asked the group to appear on his KPFK radio show. From there, having established some kind of rapport with the group, he became first their publicist, and then their manager. He had already, according to Nick Kent in *New Musical Express,* frequently brought up the subject of his past achievements, which were supposed to include winning a Pulitzer Prize for an NBC documentary on the Ku Klux Klan, and being a regular contributor to a high-brow magazine called *Psychology Today.*

The group were considerably impressed with Rieley. They needed strong direction, particularly as Brian Wilson had taken to staying in bed for long periods — reportedly more than a week at a time. (Since the lack of critical appreciation following *Pet Sounds* and as a result of drug usage, Brian had been subject to acute depression which manifested itself in disturbed behavior and increasing withdrawal from the world.) As a

result, it wasn't too long before Rieley was virtually in command of the group's strategy, which badly needed a shot in the arm, despite their appearance at Monterey. The group started playing benefit concerts, something they had never really considered previously, and began to develop a political conscience. In May 1971, they played before an audience of half a million at a May Day demonstration in Washington, and later that year canceled some paying dates to perform a benefit for the defense fund of some political prisoners.

Perhaps more significant in musical terms, they jammed on stage with the Grateful Dead at the Fillmore East in New York, from which a joint version of *Johnny B. Goode* was recorded — but not released. One of the audience at the Fillmore was Bob Dylan, who reportedly enthused over the performance. The comeback was definitely under way, and some of the credit was due to Jack Rieley, whose clear vision had fixed on this method of restoring the group's long-lost credibility in the eyes of the American record buyer.

By this time, a new album was due,

which Rieley decided should be concerned with natural conservation and ecology, subjects close to the headlines and to the consciousness of a great many people. The album was due to be called *Landlocked,* but then destiny took a hand with the re-emergence of one of the most famous 'lost' songs from *Smile.* This was *Surf's Up,* which Brian had performed solo on Leonard Bernstein's TV show. It was resurrected, and became the title track of the new Beach Boys album. Since the time that it had failed to come out on *Smile,* the track had become legendary, spoken of in hushed tones by people who had never heard it.

Two main stories exist concerning the track's resurgence, the 'official' explanation being that Brian, in a typically illogical move, suddenly decided that the track should be heard. Perhaps a more feasible explanation is that Jack Rieley decided the inclusion of *Surf's Up,* particularly as the title track, would give the group's new album a running start.

Rieley is alleged to have searched out the tape of Brian's performance on

60

the Bernstein show, and given it to the rest of the group. They, being probably more aware of the song's eminence, felt that to record it would be a master stroke, although there are reports that Brian was visibly upset by the possibility that the track might be used, and pleaded that it should remain a secret. It is possible that Brian didn't want the track to surface because, at that point, it was the only example from his best creative period that remained unheard, and perhaps he wasn't sufficiently confident of the song's inherent quality to risk it being consigned to the realms of 'has beens' in the event of an adverse public reception. Whatever the truth, his brothers decided to use the song.

Surf's Up

Van Dyke Parks, talking to *Rolling Stone*, had no doubt that the song which he co-wrote with Brian would be a success: "If they call that album *Surf's Up*, they can pre-sell 150,000 copies." Which is more or less what happened – the critics overwhelmingly gave the album their thumbs up, and it sailed into the charts, albeit not for too long. But the title track wasn't by any means the only one to attract attention – at least five of the other nine songs have been dwelt upon in various ways. For example, Bruce Johnston's magnificent *Disney Girls (1957)* is now regarded as something of a standard, and has been covered successfully on LPs by Art Garfunkel, the Captain and Tennille and Johnny Mathis, and there's even a predictable Ray Conniff version.

The album included Mike Love's adaptation of the old Robins' (later to become the Coasters) song *Riot In Cell Block Number 9*. Mike's version rejoiced in the title of *Student Demonstration Time;* it contributed to the new 'aware' Beach Boy image and became a stage highlight for the next few years.

Carl Wilson's two songs – which are effectively his first as a major writer – were both adapted a little by Jack Rieley. One of them, *Feel Flows,* was even chosen by several critics as the best track on the record and when you consider the care with which Carl recorded and produced it, such acclaim seems well deserved.

"I played piano first, and then organ. I played the piano twice, overdubbed it, and used a variable speed oscillator to make the track different speeds so that the piano would be a little bit out of tune, sort of a spread sound, that makes the piano sound like the effect of a 12-string guitar . . . that real ringing sound. Then I put the organ on, and put it through the moog at the same time, so that one side of the stereo had

the direct organ sound, and the other side had the return through the synthesizer. Then I put on the bass guitar, and then the moog . . . we put on the bells . . . percussion, and I sang on it. I put the guitar on about the same time. Then, I think it was the next day, Charles Lloyd came by and we did the flutes and saxophone . . . It was really a thrill for me to have him play on it, because he's a gifted musician. And then, the next session we did the vocals, the background part, and that was it."

Rieley was also involved as Brian's writing partner on a track called *A Day In The Life Of A Tree*, which boasted vocal contributions from both Rieley and Van Dyke Parks (who returned briefly to the fold as the co-writer of *Surf's Up*). Rieley had definitely made his mark on the album, both conceptually (*Rolling Stone* described it as "almost a concept album in its near obsession with water"), and in the more practical aspects of writing and performance. The fame of the Beach Boys was starting to return.

Unfortunately, the going wasn't all downhill yet. During the recording of *Surf's Up*, late '70/early '71, Dennis had an accident. He injured his hand, reportedly during an unsuccessful tussle with a chainsaw, although such a tool would surely have severed a limb! It was not the only version circulating about the cause of the injury – another suggested it was inflicted during a bar room brawl. In *New Musical Express*, several years after the event, Dennis supplied his own account.

"I got drunk . . ." he said. "Walked into the house, threw off my wife's clothes, ripped mine off. It was cold, and I went to slam the door, only we'd just moved and I'd forgotten that the door was made of glass, and I put my hand right through it. You know how it is when you're drunk. Barbara saved my life by putting a tourniquet on it . . . The doctor told me if I followed his instructions, I'd be using my hand again in two to three years. I was playing piano again in six months – I really worked at it. My hand literally didn't work at first. It felt weird making love, touching someone and not feeling anything, but it all came back, just like the doctor said it would, except for the two little fingers. Way down by the bone I can feel them, but that's all."

With Dennis out of commission, it was fortunate for the Beach Boys that they had a ready-made replacement. A couple of years before, while touring South Africa, they had come across a group called Flame. It was a promising band, but one which could hardly be expected to achieve full potential in a country whose apartheid laws categorized the members as 'non-white'. The Beach Boys, on the lookout for talent to sign to the Brother label (first time round), persuaded Flame to move to

the States, and used them as support act on numerous occasions. They even bought a night club during the early '70s, so that the unknown band would have a chance to be showcased in Hollywood!

Flame had the dubious distinction of being the only non-Beach Boys to ever appear on Brother Records. Carl produced a single and album for them, no doubt trying to get as much production experience as possible in the knowledge that he would have to get more involved with his own group's record production. Mike Love once somewhat obliquely explained why Brother never got around to signing anyone else. "It's a glorified label deal. We spent enough time doing the Beach Boys, on tour, in the studios and stuff – why the hell were we going to spend the rest of our lives promoting and producing other people? Besides that, we didn't have the mechanics or the proper management and promotion people around us at that time . . . and so the ideas that we had to develop Brother Records, which were very good, were never translated into sound business practice.

"We never got immersed that deeply, like the Beatles [with] Apple Records . . . We said 'Well, the only way you're going to be a record company is if you have your own distribution, sales and promotion. Just making a royalty deal with a major record company to distribute a product is nothing more than a distribution deal for your production company, so you really have no mastery over your own destiny.' We saw that immediately after we'd signed it . . ."

By the time Dennis had his accident, Flame were in disarray, so it seemed reasonable to introduce the drummer, Ricky Fataar, into the Beach Boys. Mike Love told *New Musical Express* "We can play harder rock than we've ever been able to before. Ricky has been drumming since he was nine years old – he has more scope than Dennis who just maintained a steady hard beat for the vocals."

It was achieved amicably, although it did spawn an 'unconfirmed report', which was printed in at least one British music paper, that Dennis Wilson was going to leave the Beach Boys. "*Disc* understands from a close friend of the group: 'Dennis contends that he has left the group once and for all, and is setting up a production and publishing company with his father, Murry Wilson. Dennis is quite into writing and producing commercials for various products. He was in New York last week to finish negotiations with a major company.'"

That didn't happen, of course, but there is certainly evidence that Dennis began to plan, and even to record his own solo album, although it wasn't released at the time. However, for the next couple of years, Dennis contri-

buted rather less than usual on stage, occasionally playing a bit of piano, sometimes providing extra percussion, and certainly singing more than anything else. Ricky Fataar was at least an adequate replacement drummer for the Beach Boys, but his joining had effectively squashed all hopes that Flame may have had of regrouping and making other records.

The loss of Dennis as drummer was not the only line-up change the group suffered at that time. Jack Rieley, who was by now in pretty well total control, got on very well with all the group except for one member – Bruce Johnston. Bruce, in an interview, tried to explain the animosity between himself and Rieley, and also cast some new light on the saga of *Surf's Up:* "To me, *Surf's Up* is, and always has been, one big hyped-up lie! It was a false reflection of the Beach Boys, and one which Jack engineered right from the outset. Jack was just very, very

smart in that he was able to camouflage what was actually going on by making it look like Brian Wilson was more than just a visitor at those sessions. Jack made it appear as though Brian was really there all the time. You could say I rocked the boat as far as Jack was concerned."

Bruce Johnston left the Beach Boys in 1972. The rest of the group, when asked about this change of personnel, which occurred at a time when everything seemed to be going well, were defensive. Brian, asked about it by *Record World,* said: "All I know is he got into a horrible fight with Jack Rieley. Some dispute, and they got into a horrible fight, and the next day Bruce was gone." Mike Love, talking to *New Musical Express,* was a little less terse, but similarly vague. "We had a meeting and we discussed the personal problems within the group, and the relationships between the various members within the group.

Some of us had no relationship at all, and Bruce said, 'If that's the way you feel about it, maybe I should just leave – I don't want to leave, but maybe it's for the best.'

"It was very amicable. Bruce is definitely on a solo trip, he's a good solo performer, he writes fantastic songs by himself, and the time he spent writing alone isolated him from the group. He had his own interests, his own relationships with the press, and he played a game that was oblique to the Beach Boys. But now he's free to do what he pleases. The Beach Boys never threw Bruce out, he was just on a tangent that was outside the Beach Boys for so many years. His whole idea of the future is to be a songwriter and have a TV show, and it's all based on individual musical taste and individual aspirations which are fine, but not within the framework of the group."

The result of all this was that another

64

WEA

member of Flame, Blondie Chaplin, was pulled into the group to play bass, and nothing has subsequently been heard of Flame. One other ex-member of the group, Ricky Fataar's brother, who was oddly enough known as Brother Fataar, surfaced in Britain some time later, playing for a short time with a couple of second division bands and then seemed to vanish.

Bruce, on the other hand, has done very well since he left the Beach Boys – after a slow start, during which he made several guest appearances on records by such artists as Roger McGuinn and the Legendary Masked Surfers (actually Bruce, Terry Melcher and Dean Torrence), Bruce and Terry formed their own record company, the short-lived Equinox, which made records for the songwriter Barry Mann and even David Cassidy. At the same time, Bruce composed *I Write The Songs,* which was recorded to huge effect by Barry Manilow and also

Ex-Flame member, Ricky Fataar joins the Beach Boys as drummer.

covered by the Captain and Tennille. He also wrote a big American hit for the Hudson Brothers, *Rendezvous,* and another notable track for the Captain and Tennille, *Thank You Baby.* He appeared as a session singer on Elton John's highly successful *Blue Moves* LP, as well as playing on subsequent Beach Boy albums, including *Holland* and *15 Big Ones.*

His departure apparently occurred midway through the recording of the next Beach Boys album, *Carl And The Passions – So Tough,* which was eventually released in 1972. The title harks back to one of the group's early, pre-Beach Boy, names. The album is generally accepted as being the lamest Beach Boy album since the fragmented *20/20,* but in America that didn't matter too much because it was butt-ressed by the first fruits of the contractual agreement made with Capitol.

Mike Love explained it to *New Musical Express* thus: "We've bought the rights of five old albums to distribute them for seven years, plus *Smile,* the album that was never released. The thing we want to do is a combination of bringing everyone up to date and giving everyone a chance to get an old collectors' item that has been discontinued by the record company. Americans have to write to England if they want copies of albums like *Smiley Smile.* So we are going to issue the new Beach Boys album [*Carl And The Passions*] and one of the old classics in a double set, but won't charge any more money for the old album. In England, it's coming out as a single album, because we couldn't get the rights to the old albums over here."

In the event, it wasn't *Smiley Smile* which was packaged with *Carl And The Passions,* but *Pet Sounds,* and this diverted a certain amount of critical unpleasantness away from the new album. The *Rolling Stone* review in fact spent rather longer talking about the old classic than the new pretender. Much of *Carl And The Passions* was made in a rushed ten days, and frankly, it bears the mark of a project with too little thought behind it. The stand-out track is *Marcella,* a song which bears some similarity to *Help Me Rhonda,* but strangely that track wasn't chosen as a single until after the rather un-distinguished *You Need A Mess Of Help To Stand Alone* had stiffed. Both songs were Brian Wilson/Jack Rieley collaborations, and both failed as singles, although they're probably the best tracks on the album.

Mike Love, not unnaturally, was more enthusiastic about the two songs he had co-written with Al Jardine when they were on a Transcendental Meditation course in New York. The titles – straight from the mystic song-

book – are *All This Is That* and *He Come Down,* but it's unlikely that they'd figure in anyone's favorite 20 Beach Boys tracks. In addition, there are also a couple of average contributions from the two newcomers Fataar and Chaplin called *Here She Comes* and *Hold On Dear Brother.*

A new name in the credits was Daryl Dragon, who was one of several supernumaries used by the Beach Boys at this time, including Dennis Dragon and Billy Hinsche on percussion and guitar respectively. The Dragons were the children of Carmen Dragon, the man who became famous for his orchestral albums made at the Hollywood Bowl. Daryl Dragon, during his time in the Beach Boys, became known as 'Captain Keyboards', and this nickname stuck when he achieved fame as one half of the Captain and Tennille, (recipients of Bruce Johnston's song *Thank You Baby*). His wife, Toni Tennille, is also supposed to have sung onstage with the Beach Boys at some point around this time. His songwriting contributions in *Carl And The Passions* were *Make It Good* and *Cuddle Up,* both co-written with Dennis Wilson. The latter song appear-ed later on the first, highly successful, Captain and Tennille LP.

Brian Wilson wasn't completely idle through these upheavals, because he had become heavily re-involved with the interrupted career of his wife, Marilyn, and her sister Diane Rovell. You'll remember that, as the Honeys, they'd made several records that succeeded artistically but failed commercially during the '60s. Since 1963 the third group member, cousin Ginger, had fallen out, and the Rovell Sisters adopted a new name, Spring. They signed to United Artists, and made an album – *Spring* – in 1972, which was produced by Brian with engineer Stephen Desper, who had fulfilled that role for the Beach Boys for some time past. Various Beach Boys besides Brian were involved with the album, in particular Carl, who as usual played guitar, and the co-opted Billy Hinsche. A number of Beach Boy compositions were used, including a couple pre-viously recorded by their originators on *Sunflower – This Whole World* and *Forever.* But the basis of the album is the re-treading of a number of familiar songs, in much the same way as would happen four years later with *15 Big Ones.* Tracks like *Tennessee Waltz, Everybody, Superstar* and others were familiar from versions by Kay Starr, Tommy Roe and the Carpenters, but Spring brought a pleasant freshness to them and the album can be counted an artistic success. However, it totally failed to sell, and was soon deleted. (In Britain the group and the album came out under the name American Spring because of a clash with an existing group called Spring.)

Although Spring is a major contender for the title of 'highly desirable rarity,' United Artists were sufficiently discouraged to drop the group after the album. Marilyn found this action difficult to understand, she told an interviewer: "Now how can they drop somebody after only one album? But I'm glad. I mean, they worked hard for us in Europe, but over here . . ." She shouldn't have worried — the next record company to sign the girls, Columbia, passed after only one or two singles!

While Brian was thus involved, Dennis was making a film called *Two Lane Blacktop*, in which he co-starred with another notable singer, James Taylor — but the movie was not very successful.

So after regaining a good deal of their lost popularity, the Beach Boys were apparently getting nowhere fast once again. But a further career twist was imminent. In February 1972, shortly before *Carl And The Passions* was finished, the Beach Boys made a TV spectacular in Amsterdam. This followed a hugely successful concert there in 1970 when, despite being disastrously late, they were greeted by a noisy and very enthusiastic audience, who seemed, for a change, to want to hear the newer songs as well as the oldies. This made such an impression on the group that they decided that Holland would make a good base from which they would direct their European tour, and after the TV show, they began to make plans for an early return, with a view to recording there.

The first thing they checked out was the studio situation, which didn't look too hopeful. There were several places which were technically up to standard, but they were already booked so heavily in advance that there was no chance of making an album. However, by the time this fact became clear, the various people attached to the group were so keen to continue their 'holiday' in the calm of Amsterdam — almost another world compared to the smog and traffic jams of Los Angeles — that they decided on an ambitious venture. They proposed to build a very sophisticated studio in LA, then dismantle it and have it transported to Holland, where it would be reassembled in a barn that would be converted into the shell of a studio.

Put like that, the whole operation sounds deceptively simple, but in reality, the idea very nearly turned into a nightmare. Steve Moffitt, the engineer on *Carl And The Passions*, was called during mid-March, and told to get the various recording components together by the beginning of June. He started by contacting conventional manufacturers, but none of them could help him in such a short time, so it was down to building the studio equipment himself. Utilizing parts of the recording equipment which had been installed in Brian's house (and recently moved out because Marilyn wanted to live in her living room for a change!) and adding to it new, technically very advanced units, Moffitt and his friend Gordon Rudd worked shifts for 24 hours a day to meet their schedule. This meant that once the machines were assembled, there wasn't time to check everything and make sure it worked correctly. As soon as everything was assembled, it had to be dismantled and packed in special crates to be sent air freight to Amsterdam.

Parts of the studio occupied each of the four daily flights from Los Angeles to Amsterdam for four-and-a-half weeks — and on each of the three daily flights in the opposite direction, for the correction of faulty parts! Steve Moffitt flew to Amsterdam to supervise the re-assembly, but even with his knowledge of the system he had largely designed, the first attempt at getting the machines working was a total failure. That meant long days making sure that everything did finally work, and included an occasion when a tape machine billowed smoke. As if that wasn't enough, the shell in which it was being pieced together had dreadful acoustics, and required a false floor, a redesigned ceiling, completely new lighting and several other modifications. To further complicate things, finding suitable accommodation for a party that comprised around 36 adults, ten children and several dogs, necessitated scattering people around eight different locations within a 30-mile radius of Baambrugge, where the studio was situated.

Surprisingly, even the reclusive Brian decided to move to Holland with his family. And that brought its own headaches — Marilyn, their two daughters, Diane Rovell and their housekeeper went over first, leaving Brian in LA. Twice he was booked on flights to Amsterdam, but only got as far as LA airport. Perhaps that wasn't too extraordinary — since abandoning touring seven years before, Brian had rarely been outside Los Angeles, let alone abroad. At his third try, it was confirmed to the waiting party in Amsterdam that he had definitely boarded the plane, but three hours after it landed, there was no sign of him. Someone found his passport apparently abandoned on a seat in the plane, and he was eventually discovered, fast asleep in the duty free area.

After all the commotion that preceded the making of the album, it

Daryl Dragon and Toni Tennille, occasional Beach Persons!

A & M

66

Al Jardine, Mike Love, Keith Moon and Elton John, celebrate onstage in London.

wouldn't have been at all surprising if the eventual music was a complete disaster, but strangely enough, the result was much closer to a triumph. However, when the record company first heard the album, it was rejected as sub-standard. Jack Rieley had previously announced that this would be the group's first double album. Eventually, that idea was modified to a single 12-inch LP with an additional 7-inch record (also at $33\frac{1}{3}$ rpm) but even that didn't meet with the approval of the Reprise officials.

As far as they could hear, the result of a cripplingly expensive trip to another continent (estimated at a cost of about $250,000 and that may be conservative!) resulted in an average set of songs, plus a 'fairy tale' of Brian Wilson's invention on the extra smaller record. In many ways, this was a shortsighted judgment – while some of the tracks were less than exceptional, a three-part epic called *California Saga*, written by Mike Love and Al Jardine, was an excellent achievement, an emotive hymn of appreciation to the writers' birthplace, picking out the features which made it so highly desirable. The second part of the trilogy, *The Beaks Of Eagles*, was adapted from a poem by Robinson Jeffers, a man who shared John Steinbeck's

distinction of recording the sights and sounds of California so vividly as to make them familiar even to those who had never been there.

Other tracks had their merits – Carl's contribution, *The Trader*, is well-respected, one of several tracks on which Jack Rieley helped out with the lyrics. And then there's the 'fairy tale', *Mount Vernon And Fairway*. Both Mike Love and Brian Wilson talked to *Crawdaddy* about this, although their views didn't totally agree. First, Mike Love: "Ah yes, it's just like old times. I can remember that around 1957 or '58, Brian had an old Rambler, and he used to come over to my house a lot

67

to hang out and sing. I was living at the corner of Mt Vernon and Fairway in the View Park/Baldwin Hills section of Los Angeles at the time. You know that line in Brian's fairy tale about 'distant lights'? Well, that was from my bedroom upstairs, which had a fantastic view . . . We used to sleep in the bunks, and I'd have a transistor radio on under the covers so we could listen to the late night R&B on KGFJ and KDAY. You remember that part in the fairy tale about the prince's 'magic transistor radio'?

"Brian thought up the idea of the fairy tale in Holland, and we all thought it was great how the whole thing came together. We all loved working on it, and from the start we thought it made a great little 'present' to go with the album, so that's what we did."

Brian saw his conception rather differently: "Well, we were in another country, in Holland, and I just sat around and drank apple sap — that's like apple cider — and just sat around and dreamed. And one night I was listening to that Randy Newman album *Sail Away*, and I was sitting there with a pencil and started writing. And I found that if I kept playing the Randy Newman album, I could still stay in that mood. It was the weirdest thing — I wrote the whole fairy tale while listening to that album. I was thinking about Mike Love's house, and I just wrote 'There was a mansion on the hill,' and then later on, in my head, I created a fairy tale. But nobody was ready for it, nobody. I remember, Carl said 'WHAT?'

"Then I got . . . depressed, so Carl did all the editing on it, and even did part of it himself when I wasn't there. It was really a thrill, the first time we'd ever done anything that creative. I wanted it to be on the album, but they [the group] said 'No, it's too long.' We argued and all, and I was depressed. So they finally compromised by saying 'OK, we'll slip it in the package as an extra record or something.'"

There's no doubt that the fairy tale isn't to everyone's taste, but at least as many feel it to be a significant part of the Brian Wilson legend. At the time, the Reprise executives weren't convinced, and in desperation, contacted several of Brian's one-time collaborators to see whether they'd heard even a snatch of some new song which Brian was writing, which could be included to 'rescue' the album. Van Dyke Parks came up with the answer, a cassette of a new song called *Sail On Sailor*, although the capture of this song was not without its problems. Apparently, the verse was soon complete, but Van Dyke had to convince Brian strongly, almost to the point of bullying him, to write the middle eight section of the song. The final credits for the song include Brian, Van Dyke Parks, and another friend, Tandyn Almer (who had written the

Association's huge hit *Along Comes Mary*) composing the music and Jack Rieley and Ray Kennedy writing the words. This massive collaboration seemed to do the trick, and the album came out to far greater critical acclaim (and, more important, sold more) than *Carl And The Passions*.

Around the time that *Sail On Sailor* was being recorded for *Holland* (the obvious title for the album) in LA, several of the Beach Boys helped out on an album, *Waves*, by reed player Charles Lloyd. He had contributed some overdubs on *Holland* (and played an important role in Carl's *Feel Flows* on *Surf's Up*). Doubtless one of the main reasons they decided to help Charles Lloyd was because the

Dennis in 'Two Lane Blacktop'.

main track on which they appear is called *TM*. Mike, Al, Carl and Billy Hinsche (the latter by now an auxiliary member of the group) provided most of the vocals on the track, which also has Roger McGuinn playing his trademark 12-string guitar.

The Beach Boys and Rieley parted company during 1973, and he apparently settled in Holland, where much of his best work with the group had been achieved. There can be little doubt that Rieley played a major part in helping the Beach Boys to rediscover their potential, and in many ways, his role in their revitalization seems to have been underrated subsequently.

But for the Wilson brothers Rieley's departure was a minor trauma in comparison to their father's death on June 4, 1973. According to his wife, Audree, Murry had had a heart attack earlier in the year, and knew that he was close to death. He'd even told Dennis that his end wasn't far away, having oddly

70

enough established a closer relationship with this most errant of his sons than with Carl or Brian. Carl, predictably, was the brother who took the loss with most equanimity, until he discovered that Brian was not going to attend the funeral, whereupon he was furious, until Audree calmed him. The group put out a press release concerning Murry, and even Bruce Johnston took a small advertisement in at least one British music paper saying that Murry would be missed. Not long afterwards, Brian was interviewed by *Record World,* while in New York with Diane Rovell, and asked if his visit was purely for promotional reasons, as Spring had just signed their deal with Columbia. He said "Well, no. The real reason we're here is that my father died two weeks ago. I went through a little bit of a change. I'm not using that as a reason for being here now, but that's one of them. I haven't been feeling too good because he died, you know. I went through a shock, and I wanted to leave town."

So once again, the Beach Boys hit a series of personal and business setbacks just as everything seemed to be going right. Their record company wasn't too pleased with them either — since they'd signed with Reprise, there had only been four albums in four years, and none of them had sold sufficiently well to go gold. Neither had there been any hit singles for a considerable period. And even Brian was giving cause for concern again with his unpredictable behavior. At about this time he jumped on stage at the Troubadour in Los Angeles to 'jam' with Larry Coryell. That wouldn't have been too bad, except for the fact that he was wearing pyjamas and a dressing gown, and insisted on singing an old Gene Vincent song, which was emphatically not what Coryell was playing at the time.

The answer to all these problems was a double live album. In fact, a particularly good one entitled *In Concert.* In some ways, the album comes across as rather a self-effacing package, although whether that's the fault of the group or the record company isn't too clear. Certainly, the sleeve only lists half the tracks, as if there were some reason for concealing what is in the other half of the set. One critic, in *New Musical Express,* despite giving the album a very good review, commented that "Dennis Wilson appears to do virtually nothing, Al Jardine . . . probably doesn't even have his guitar plugged in . . . and big brother Brian Wilson was nowhere to be seen when the tracks were recorded." To add to the difficulties, Reprise nearly didn't accept *In Concert.* The company rejected it as a single album and very nearly rejected it as a double. Perhaps a rejection would have finally broken the Beach Boys up.

A measure of the group's lack of

plans, joining Joe Walsh's Barnstorm group, which was formed in 1974 after Walsh left the James Gang. It seems likely that the two ex-Flame members were somewhat neglected as a result of the group not having a real manager at the time, and also because they had been introduced by the since-departed Jack Rieley. Although in many ways the two had never properly fitted in with the Beach Boys, their departure brought on another series of crises.

The band now desperately needed a guitarist/bass player and a drummer, two essential components in a group which was relying a great deal on live performances. The vacancy for a bass player was filled by the unlikely figure of James William Guercio, whose previous fame had been as a remarkably successful producer. He had been the genius behind the astounding success of the group Chicago, and he also successfully produced Blood, Sweat and Tears and the Buckinghams, among others, as well as owning the noted Caribou Studios in Colorado. Guercio, like several of his predecessors, claimed to have been a long-time fan of the Beach Boys, and began to take care of some of the administrative aspects of the group, as well as becoming their bass player for a while.

That was the first vacancy taken care of, by which time the second had appeared. Dennis Wilson, who had taken a decreasing part in live performance, was cajoled into re-adopting his previous position behind the drums. While Dennis could hardly be described as a drum artist, the man he replaced, Ricky Fataar, described his technique to *New Musical Express* as follows: "He's not into being flashy. He can't roll or do fancy frills, but he *can* play . . . out a backbeat, which is what their old records are all about."

So, late in 1974, everything seemed to be back in reasonable shape, with a complete group. In the meantime, something considerably more significant had occurred, a development which was to zoom them right back up to the top of the tree. It was as if, to borrow a surfing phrase, they had found a new, and perfect, wave. Soon after *In Concert* was released — containing as it did a selection of oldies, many of them dating back to the group's surf sound of the early '60s, and with only one completely new track, the rather lame *We Got Love* — Capitol Records took a fresh look at the potential gold in their vaults. They decided that some repackaging might be in order. After all, many people had justifiably said that the live double's success was due more to the inclusion of *Help Me Rhonda, California Girls, Surfin' USA* and *Fun, Fun, Fun* than to *Marcella, Sail On Sailor* and *The Trader*. So they got together a package which was called *Endless Summer*, and a new era commenced.

direction at this point is that some of the tracks were over a year old when they were released, due to no acceptable material being available. There's conceivably some connection between this lack of activity and the fact that by the time the package was released, Blondie Chaplin had left the band.

Mike Love, talking to *Sounds* around the time of the album's release in early 1974, was suitably vague about Blondie's departure, and similarly enthusiastic about the live album. "He's no longer with us. I don't know what he's doing now — he's a really good guitar player, but he'd been unhappy for some time. But the live album is good. We wanted to get something on there from all the different eras of the Beach Boys, and I think it worked out well in being a very representative album. You get almost the total feeling of a concert, except that the crowd noise gets mixed down a bit. Obviously on a live record there are points where we could have done a solo better, but that's only to be expected."

To tie up the loose ends as far as Blondie Chaplin goes is difficult — Bruce Johnston, a couple of years later, indicated that Blondie had been offered several recording deals, but at that time hadn't accepted them, and it was not until 1977 that his first record since leaving the Beach Boys — an album simply titled *Blondie Chaplin* — was released in America on Elektra/Asylum. Blondie's final recorded appearance with the Beach Boys was on the *In Concert* album, and that was the first album that the group had made since leaving Capitol five years before that achieved gold status. Even then, a Reprise executive said that it wouldn't have qualified if it hadn't been a double LP, because gold albums are awarded for achieving a total income rather than units sold, and *In Concert*, being a double LP, was more expensive than a normal single album.

Not long afterwards, the other 'outsider', Ricky Fataar, also left the group, although he had much more concrete

73

Do It Again
1975-77

WEA

Before 1974, there had been a good many Beach Boys compilations released on both sides of the Atlantic. The *Best Of* series had reached Volume 3, there had been a *Greatest Hits*, not to mention a considerable number of reissues and repackaging. It wasn't as if the early tracks, from the start up to 1965 – the *Summer Days (And Summer Nights)* album – weren't available, but someone at Capitol decided it was about time for another exploitation of the back catalog, particularly in view of the partial renaissance which had occurred with the *Holland* LP.

Endless Summer

The result was a 20-track album, a double LP in the States, a single LP in England, although with exactly the same tracks, called *Endless Summer*. It was heavily advertised on TV and went platinum rapidly. That means it sold one million units, and was probably the very first of the group's albums to have done so well, and certainly the first Beach Boys LP for a decade or more to have topped the charts. As *Record World*, an American trade paper put it, "In a move virtually unprecedented in recent industry history, a repackaged album set by a group with no current hits has attained the number 1 spot on the *Record World* album chart. Capitol released this repackage of early Beach Boys material in July, and it has steadily climbed the chart, reaching its current position after nine weeks. The story of the rise of this album is one which tells still another chapter in the value of television advertising on record sales."

Interestingly, there are various claims that the Beach Boys individually or collectively helped their old company with the repackage – *Record World* indicated that Brian Wilson had been involved in choosing the tracks, and that he had also conceived the title of *Endless Summer*, but more recently Mike Love was adamant that he was the one who deserved the credit. "I met with Capitol Records on *Endless Summer* . . . but the fact of the matter is I hoped they'd do an anthological approach rather than *20 Great Goldies* or something, and so we got 80% of the way there. The artwork was, I thought, meager to say the most about it . . . it could have been done a lot better . . . *Endless Summer*, the very title itself, that was the title I gave it, is better than *20 Golden Moldies*, because to me it implies two of the most important qualities of the Beach Boys – timelessness, the eternal quality of the music, and summer – *Endless Summer*."

At around the same time, Reprise also had a Beach Boys double album on the market in America, a repackage

of *Wild Honey* and *20/20*, but it didn't stand a chance next to a wall-to-wall hits package, although it did do fairly well in the charts. Yet again, the public of America had demonstrated that they were probably more interested in the early work of the Beach Boys, which could be so easily assimilated, than their more adventurous and complicated later records. *In Concert*, which had contained a modicum of oldies, had gone gold, the first Beach Boys album to do that well for Warner/Reprise, and now *Endless Summer* sold in immense quantities.

This big nostalgia boom didn't particularly please Brian. Talking to *Rolling Stone* in 1976, he said "The Capitol albums bugged me. I hate those old falsettos, I really do, and it's embarrassing since I've grown up. They just packaged them and I guess they've sold better than anything we've done in a while. We grew up with it, we were a product of all that. There was surfing and California girls and cars, that was California. I don't relate to that, to the whole California thing, anymore."

All this chart activity precipitated a bizarre struggle between the group's old and new record companies – after the *Wild Honey & 20/20* package slipped down, Warner/Reprise put out another double repackage, this time of *Friends* and *Smiley Smile*, which made the charts for a few weeks, but still in no way matched *Endless Summer*. Capitol were undoubtedly coming out on top, and a measure of this was that at a presentation of gold and platinum albums to the Beach Boys for *Endless Summer*, Steve Love, Mike's brother and a managerial aide to the group, issued a statement which tersely said, "We'd like to see Warner Brothers Records make the same kind of magnificent effort to sell our records that Capitol has made so that more and more people will be able to hear and enjoy our music." A damning indictment and a change of tune which Capitol must have appreciated after years of criticism from the Beach Boys!

It was around this time – towards the end of 1974 – that another shot in the arm occurred for the Beach Boys. Their bass player at this point was James William Guercio, who was also taking care of some of the management duties for the group, as well as being indispensable to Chicago, the group with whom he made his name. It must have occurred to Guercio that to put a road show together featuring both the groups in which he had an interest would be an astounding success, so that's what he did. Chicago, despite being a continual target for critical sniping throughout most of the '70s, possessed an incredibly strong and loyal following among record buyers, and with the Beach Boys having just achieved a number

1 album, Guercio reckoned on pulling in the crowds. And they certainly did – a 12-city tour grossed over $7 million. In addition a single by Chicago called *Wishing You Were Here* – which consisted largely of the Beach Boys singing, with the big brassy sound of Chicago behind them – went Top 10 in America, and might have done similarly well in Britain had it not been for the enormous British apathy towards Chicago at the time.

For undisclosed reasons, Guercio and the Beach Boys discontinued their business relationship towards the end of 1975, but not before three more significant events had occurred. The first of these was the release (and almost immediate withdrawal) of a Beach Boys Christmas single, *Child Of Winter*. It was a partial reversion to old style Beach Boys – a simple enough song aimed at children who still hang up their stockings, and with a large slice of the well-known Xmas song *Here Comes Santa Claus* in the middle. It's great, but there was a major problem attached to it which both prevented it becoming the hit it undoubtedly should have been, and has now granted it the status of collector's item. Yes, another Beach Boys collector's item!

The problem was that Brian Wilson didn't finish the record until the middle of December, 1974, and it's a known and very reasonable fact in the industry that Christmas discs have to be put out in October to build up sales. Thus, when *Child Of Winter* was released two days *after* Christmas, it got very little radio play, and the limited pressing which Warner Brothers had undertaken soon ran out. Strangely enough, the record nearly came out in Britain a couple of years later – a chart shot for Christmas 1976 – but despite the single being pressed, it was never released.

The B-side of the record – an Al Jardine song called *Susie Cincinatti* – also has an interesting history. It had originally been released as the B-side of a track from *Sunflower*, in 1970, but only in America. After that, it nearly made an appearance as the running mate of *Child Of Winter*, on the unreleased British version and when that didn't happen, it finally made it into British shops in 1976 as the second track on side two of *15 Big Ones*.

Susie Cincinatti was a song based on a real person, a lady taxi driver whom the group first encountered in 1968. Her name was Joellyn Lambert and she was rediscovered in 1976 as a result of the group placing newspaper advertisements asking *Susie*, as the inspiration behind the song, to be their guest at a concert in Cincinatti eight years after that first meeting. Al Jardine told *Rolling Stone* "It was a rainy night, about 11 pm, and in those days we didn't use limousines. We got

76

this lady cabdriver and she was kind of unusual — there weren't many lady cabdrivers then, especially at that time of night. It was Carl, Dennis and me, and she was telling us a few things about herself. She looked like a worker, and was chunky, to say the least." Joellyn, in the same article, admitted that at the time she'd have never heard of the Beach Boys, although it was possible that one of her seven children might have.

After the aborted release of *Child Of Winter* it was time again for Capitol to flex their creative muscles, which they did with another double album, this time with the 23-tracked *Spirit Of America*. Although the cream of their early catalog had been used on *Endless Summer*, there were still good numbers available, and, more to the point, worthwhile. And, as an added bonus, Capitol were able to include a 1969 hit, *Break Away*. Although much of the post-*Pet Sounds* material had been leased to Brother/Reprise, it had been in the form of complete albums, and *Break Away* had for some reason never appeared on an album. *Spirit Of America* went plati-

Golden days for 'Endless Summer'.

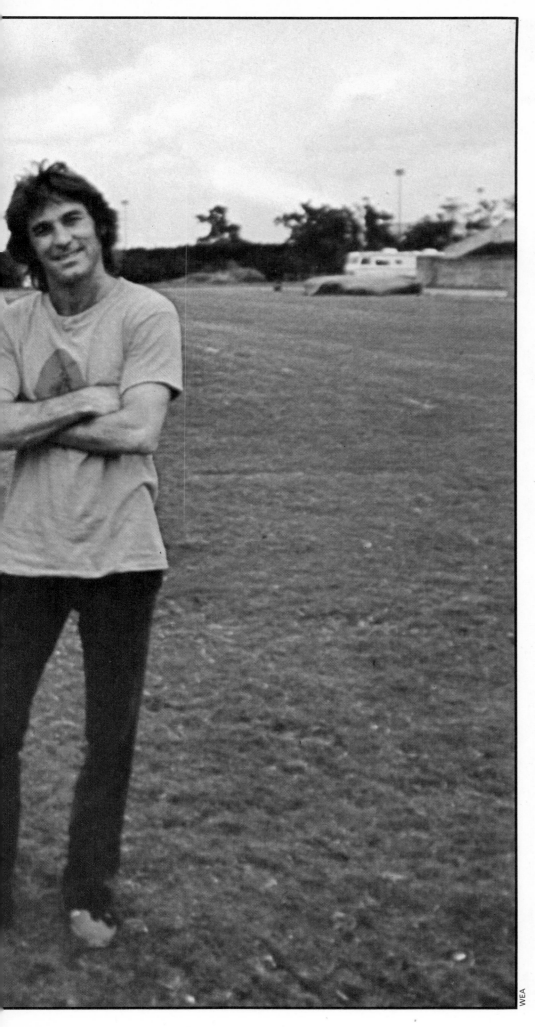

num, like *Endless Summer*. Apparently, this time the group were not consulted about the release, but as Mike Love said "I approved of the fact that it sold a million." The Capitol reissue program was still proving both a success and an embarrassment for the Beach Boys because, by mid-1975, it had been two years since *Holland*, their last original album.

In the summer of that year, the group went to England, specifically to Wembley Stadium, where they were due to play in a huge Midsummer Day concert, listed second below Elton John but above Rufus, Joe Walsh and the Eagles. The stadium was officially full up with 72,000 people, although there seemed to be double that number around. It was a hot June day, and the level of excitement peaked at six o'clock in the evening, with the sun still high, when the Beach Boys came on stage.

They were ideal for the occasion, as was proved when many thousand voices helped them out in raucous, word-perfect, unison on all but five of the 22 songs they played. (Those five were all post-Capitol numbers – *Surf's Up*, *Sail On Sailor*, *The Trader* and *Cool Water*, plus a Dennis Wilson hymn to California, *You Are So Beautiful*.) Without moving a muscle, Capitol Records had received another huge plug for their products but the scant attention paid to the handful of newer songs must have rung alarm bells in Beach Boy brains. And this despite the fact that every journalist in the stadium, plus a large part of the crowd, would tell you that the Beach Boys blew Elton John, the star of the show, about ten miles off stage. It must be noted that Elton, slightly over-reaching himself, had decided to play the whole of his then brand new *Captain Fantastic* LP to an audience who couldn't possibly have been familiar with it. Coming after a solid hour of Beach Boys classics, he didn't have a chance, but that in no way detracts from the group's performance, which was pure magic.

Jim Guercio moved away from the group during late '75 leaving them in a very strange position. They had lately achieved two platinum albums, played to vast crowds in several countries, and were arguably at a peak of popularity never previously approached. Yet they hadn't produced an original LP for two and a half years, and were at loggerheads with their record company because of the fact, and because there didn't seem any immediate prospect of the situation improving. They couldn't keep relying on old material and the Beach Boys' career was starting to look dead. What was needed was the return of the man who had first engineered the group's rise to fame, particularly through his enormous songwriting talent. It was time for Brian to come to the rescue.

But what had Brian, whose behavior was still unpredictable, been doing since *Holland*? Well, not a lot — Steve Love told *People* magazine that Brian's compositions account for an astonishing 94% of the group's revenue, and that they had sold more than 80 million records, so from a financial viewpoint, there didn't seem much need for Brian to work — except perhaps to put down something he really liked, something like *Child Of Winter*, perhaps. But oddly that didn't seem to be the case. Despite his vast earnings from royalties, stories began to proliferate about Brian never having any money, arriving at people's houses and asking their owners to pay cab drivers.

Part of the reason for this financial embarrassment seems to have been uncovered by Tim White in *Crawdaddy*, talking with Brian's brother Carl: "I know there was a thing where Brian kept on giving people money to score [drugs]. Not for himself, but for themselves. It's like he was giving a guy every week a few hundred bucks, and a very well known guy at that."

White also received a quote from an anonymous friend, who used to dine with Brian during 1975. "Brian seems to have a problem getting spending money, and he would ask me if he could borrow $80. I'd always give it to him, but after a few times, I started to wonder why the hell Brian Wilson, who's made millions of dollars in the record business, didn't have any money of his own. I couldn't understand it."

This embarrassing lack of cash seems to be the only logical reason why Brian signed a production contract in 1975 with Equinox, the company run by Terry Melcher and Bruce Johnston. According to Tim White in *Crawdaddy*, the contract called for Brian to produce 36 tracks, with no time limit as to when this should happen. For signing that contract, Brian received an advance of $23,000, plus what Bruce Johnston called "probably the highest production royalty any producer has ever received."

One source maintained that at around this time, Brian wanted to sever his connections with the Beach Boys. Obviously that didn't come to pass and Brian's contract with Equinox didn't exactly come to pass either, at least, not in the way that Melcher and Johnston had no doubt hoped. At the time of writing, only two tracks made

for that company had any connection with Brian, and they were remakes of oldies — *Why Do Fools Fall In Love* (which the Beach Boys had covered many years before on *Shut Down Volume 2*) and *Money Honey*. The artists involved were called California Music, actually a collective title for Bruce Johnston, Terry Melcher, Dean Torrence and a few others including Brian, who had recorded previously as the Legendary Masked Surfers.

Terry Melcher told *Crawdaddy* that Brian, having begun work on the tracks, suddenly refused to finish them. "He wouldn't go all the way. He wouldn't even touch anything in the control booth — he acted like he was afraid to. He'd offer suggestions, but he wouldn't go near the board. He knows his reputation, so he makes a lot of unfinished records. Sometimes I feel that he feels that he's peaked and doesn't want to put his stamp on records so that peers will have a Brian Wilson record to criticize." Eventually, *Why Do Fools Fall In Love* was released, but didn't attract any chart attention, and *Money Honey* seems to have been forgotten.

Brian produced nothing else for Equinox and it may be quite un-

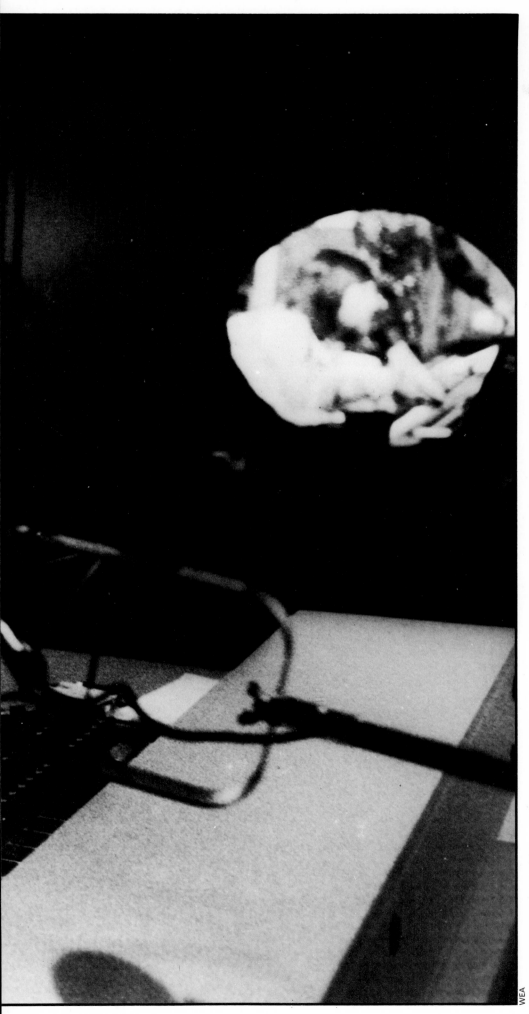

connected, but the company ground to a halt. (Johnston became a solo performer and Melcher apparently returned to production after a brief stint as an artist.) In many ways, it may be fortuitous that Brian's deal with Equinox bore no fruit, because if we're to believe the stories of financial problems, it persuaded him to return to producing, writing and even singing for the Beach Boys.

Before then Brian had appeared as a vocalist on a couple of tracks put out by well-known artists with whom he had no previous connection. One was Johnny Rivers, a veteran hit-maker who seems to have the ability, like John Mayall, to discover and attract extremely talented help to make his records special. The track in which Brian Wilson was concerned is no exception — it was a remake of the old Beach Boys hit *Help Me Rhonda*, and who better to sing the harmonies? The result was a big hit. The other track was less successful — both Brian and Marilyn helped out on the backup vocals of a song called *Boat To Sail*, written and sung by Jackie De Shannon. In the second verse of the song, it is rumored that Ms De Shannon changed an original lyric of 'California songs are never left behind' to 'Brian Wilson songs are never left behind,' which is how it eventually appeared, causing Brian acute embarrassment.

Just the appearance of Brian in recording studios after his very long absence was a very hopeful sign. Once again, things were on an upward slant, and were helped along by yet another Capitol compilation released in Britain, with a title which Mike Love must have disliked, *20 Golden Greats.* While it inevitably contained material which had appeared many times before, some of it on *Endless Summer*, it was a much more representative *Best Of* than anything previously released anywhere because it contained some of the later Capitol recordings which the company had not leased to Reprise in the UK. With the benefit of an enormous television advertising campaign, it had no difficulty in going straight to the top of the chart, and earning awards in several kinds of precious metal. While it was yet another way of emphasizing that the Beach Boys were back near the top, it also emphasized the problem of getting out something original — by now, it was close to three years since *Holland*, and after such a gap almost any other group would have been forgotten.

Although it has never been detailed, Carl, Dennis, Mike and Al must have worked hard to persuade Brian to help them cut a new album. His involvement now became a necessity. There had been mentions at various times during 1974 and '75 that a new studio album was in preparation and it may be presumed that without Brian's genius, the results were ordinary. Dennis Wilson, quoted in *Crawdaddy*, said "Brian Wilson is the Beach Boys. He is the band. We're his . . . messengers. He is all of it, period. We're nothing, he's everything." While that may seem a bit strong, the statistics about Brian being responsible for 94% of the Beach Boys revenue certainly gives credence to such sentiments.

15th Big One

During the first half of 1976, the reunited original Beach Boys went into the Brother Records studio in Santa Monica, a building so anonymous that even the kids who work nearby had no idea what the place was. The intention was to get a new album together, and in order to achieve that a little more easily, it was decided to include a number of oldies. It was felt that this would enable Brian to refamiliarize himself with the studio by producing songs that he knew, without the responsibility of having to create new masterpieces. As he told *Rolling Stone*, "I personally ran out of ideas and turned to some old stuff, and thought, hey, for the time being, it's cool just to do old ones. There's not a lot of new stuff." Around the same time, he also told Associated Press, "There is going to be basic disapproval [when the album comes out]. People will say the group copped out of the writing derby." To *Crawdaddy*, he said "I looked at the guys and they looked kinda sad. They didn't look happy, they looked like something was wrong. I said to myself 'Hey, maybe they're upset because we're not having any hit singles! Maybe they're mad at me!' I checked into it, and sure enough, as soon as we did *Palisades Park* [one of the oldies on the album], everybody was happy again."

The album, called *15 Big Ones*, was released in the latter half of 1976. The title is said to refer both to the number of tracks on the record and also the number of years the Beach Boys had been together. Many critics, having experienced media saturation about this new burst of energy from Brian, were frankly disappointed with the record, but to put it into perspective, this was the most work Brian had contributed to any Beach Boys album since the '60s. As a result, if *15 Big Ones* was a failure, it was, at least, an honorable one.

Eight of the tracks were oldies; in addition there were two tracks from the past — *Susie Cincinatti* (which included contributions from Bruce Johnston and Daryl and Dennis Dragon) and *It's OK*, with some of the drumming by Ricky Fataar, and

Back together in New York.

saxophone from Britain's Roy Wood. That only leaves five tracks which had to be done from scratch, of which Brian Wilson wrote two, and co-wrote two others. It was a new album, but not necessarily an original one. Brian was working under enormous pressure, not only from his siblings, but from personal problems which involved him in psychological treatment. It was even rumored in *People* magazine that some of the vocals Brian provided on the album were of such poor quality that the rest of the group were forced to sneak into the studio after he had gone home to re-record them. The strain was enormous, and so, apparently, was Brian, who had put on so much weight that he was turning the scales at around 240 lbs (approximately 17 stone).

The story of Brian's treatment under clinical psychologist, Dr Eugene Landy, was recounted at some length in a late 1976 edition of *Rolling Stone*. Marilyn Wilson: "The thing that made me go to Dr Landy was I couldn't stand to see Brian, whom I just love and adore, unhappy with himself and not really creating. Because music is his whole life, that's number one to him. So one of my girlfriends told me about Dr Landy, and I went and talked to him for an hour. I said 'I need someone who's gonna go to him, not where he had to go to you, because he won't do it.' And Dr Landy said 'Yeah, I think I can do it.' When I met Dr Landy, I knew I'd met someone who could play Brian's game." After a period of pretending that Landy was actually visiting the Wilson house to work on Marilyn's problems, eventually Brian asked for a consultation, and the 'course' was under way.

Landy's reputation as a 'showbiz shrink', with a scale of charges which were self-confessedly "outrageously expensive," seems, according to various reports, to have centered around Brian losing weight by dieting and exercising, and by finally having some external discipline applied to his life. Landy, explaining to *Rolling Stone* what he considered to be Brian's problems, said "He wasn't relating on the level in society where we have expectancies of what we expect people to do. When you pick the phone up, [you are expected] to say hello. If you do something different, depending on how different, you frighten people around you. And if you're frightened yourself, you simply withdraw." Apparently, this kind of behavior was affecting those around Brian more than it was worrying him, and certainly a number of reports have indicated that he didn't behave in very predictable ways.

Brian, also interviewed in *Rolling Stone*, seemed pretty much in agreement with this diagnosis, although he

felt that the basic idea of the program was "to correct me from taking drugs . . . Up until four months ago I was taking a lot of cocaine. And these doctors came in and showed me a way to stop doing it, which is having bodyguards with you all the time so you can't get to it . . . That approach works because there's someone right there all the time — it keeps you on the spot. They catch you when you're ready to do something you shouldn't do. It works until you have finally reached the stage where you don't need it anymore."

It doesn't quite end with that simplistic, and somewhat 'cold turkey' style of cure. "They teach me socialization, how to socialize. They're just teaching me different social graces, like manners . . . I did [have them], but I lost them. Drugs took 'em away . . . I got real paranoid, I couldn't do anything.

"I was unhappy as all heck. I knew I was screwing myself up, and I couldn't do anything about it. I was a useless little vegetable. I made everybody very angry at me because I wasn't able to work, to get off my butt. Coke every day. Goin' over to parties. Just havin' bags of snow around, just snortin' it down like crazy . . .

"The way I deal with it is I go jogging in the morning. I goddam get out of bed and I jog, and I make sure I stay in shape. That's how I do it. And so far the only way I've been keeping from drugs is with those bodyguards, and the only way I've been going jogging is those bodyguards have been taking me jogging."

It was at this point in the *Rolling Stone* interview that Brian is quoted as asking the author, David Felton, whether he could provide some kind of drug or knew where Brian could score. This was a fairly definite indica-

tion that the problems still persisted, and that the treatment was only finding partial success. This was confirmed by British rock star Dave Edmunds in *Melody Maker.* Talking about an evening spent at the Wilson house he said "It was a bit strange actually. Always wanted to meet him, but it was, well, very uncomfortable. Very weird. This 'Brian's back!' business — he's not. Musically, he's still got it. He sat at the piano and played some beautiful things, but when it comes to conversation, nothing."

Brian did seem, however, to be making a concerted attempt to come to terms with reality. As well as taking a much more active part in the studio, he also went back on the road with the Beach Boys at the end of 1976. He played some important concerts with the group, like three nights at Madison Square Garden during November, and a December 31 concert at the Forum

in Los Angeles. This marked the 15th anniversary of the Beach Boys' first major concert way back in 1961. Apparently, these weren't simply one-off occurrences; the intention was to continue live concerts as Brian told *Sounds* during February 1977. "I do feel more like a member again now, and it's a little easier to cope. I played about 35 shows last year. It was a little scary to be out there, but it was very productive, and the group worked hard together. I was just thrilled to be part of it. The group's very positive about it. They act a lot more positive than they ever have before, especially about doing tours and everything like that. The boys believe in themselves, they believe they have something good to offer people, and they're doing their job."

Talk of working at the job also came up in the same interview in the context of Dr Landy's occupational therapy for

Brian. Landy ''took me to the studio, and put me on a program of songwriting. He just said 'I want you to write songs. That's your job in life, you're supposed to write songs, and you might as well just sit down and start writing songs.' I said 'Alright, I'll give it a try,' so I sat down and I wrote a song a day for 14 or 15 days.''

Brian also spoke of the problems he had been experiencing with songwriting to *Rolling Stone:* ''Lately I have found it difficult as heck to finish a song. It's a funny thing. Probably not much of a song left in me . . . if any, because I've written so many, some 250 songs or 300 or whatever it is. And the creativity just doesn't seem as vast . . . That's why we did a lot of oldies but goodies this time on our album [*15 Big Ones*]. That got us going, as a matter of fact.

''I meditate, and also I *think* about meditation, which is funny. I think

that's gonna be the answer. As it progresses, I think that I'm going to gather more peace of mind, I'll be able to gather my thoughts a little easier. I won't be as jangled in the nerves. I think it's going to aid my creativity.'' Brian admitted to having ''a writing block right now,'' but the general tone was optimistic. Slowly, and painfully, one of rock's true geniuses was clawing his way back.

So in 1976, the five original Beach Boys got back together. A great deal had happened to each one of them in the 15 years since they had spent their food money on hiring instruments. Take Al Jardine, for instance — after living in the environs of Los Angeles most of his life, he moved north, apparently to escape the ambience of Southern California, and took up residence with his wife Lynda in Big Sur, near Monterey, where they breed Arabian horses on a 75-acre ranch.

Unlike the rest of the group, Al feels ''the music is just a stepping stone to personal pleasure,'' which seems to consist of being at home with Lynda and their two boys — Matthew and Adam — and getting involved in ecological matters. He is one of the two non-Wilson members of the group who still takes an active part in Transcendental Meditation — both he and Mike are teachers of the discipline.

Love, of course, has always been the most interested TM follower among the rock star fraternity. It's been an enduring commitment through three broken marriages. His fiancée, Sue Oliver, adopted his philosophy and started studying how to teach TM. Mike's total commitment to the Maharishi and what he stands for was demonstrated early in 1977, when he took a six month sabbatical from the group to learn even more about meditation in Switzerland, nominating Dean

To mass acclaim at Wembley, the Beach Boys stole the show from Elton John.

Torrence as his substitute in the event of the Beach Boys deciding to embark on any live work.

Carl Wilson stayed much nearer home, living on the beach just outside Los Angeles with his wife Annie and their two children. His main interest remains in music, but specifically in production. Since he doesn't have to do so much of that for the Beach Boys since Brian's return, he's worked with Ricci Martin and with auxiliary Beach Boy Billy Hinsche, who is also his brother-in-law. Carl and Billy also helped out on the highly-rated first Asylum album by Warren Zevon, and Carl intended taking tuition in orchestration. This interest in formal musical theory may account for a story in *People* magazine which said that Carl went to a Rolling Stones concert in 1976, but left after only ten minutes because of the excessive noise. It's perhaps an indication that he's not

intending to take the Beach Boys into areas of heavy rock.

None of the foregoing could lead to suspicions that the Beach Boys are likely to change their style of music in the foreseeable future, and perhaps Dennis Wilson, the only member of the group who wants to move into different fields, is using his re-established solo career as a vehicle, rather than involving the rest of the group in his own experimentation. Of course, he's still into surfing, although doubtless the fact that he's now over 30 is beginning to cramp his style somewhat, and he also lists his hobbies as fishing and gardening — two strangely unathletic activities for the Beach Boy who was always on the go. Dennis is also on his third marriage, the current wife being Karen Lamm, ex-wife of Chicago's keyboard player Robert Lamm. He has reportedly spent a lot of time in the Brother Records studio creating lavish

orchestrations, closer to classical than pop music in style, reflecting his admiration for classical composer Richard Wagner.

There's a large happy musical 'family' surrounding the Beach Boys. This includes Mike Love's brother Steve, who handles much of the management work required by the group, and another brother, Stan, a professional basketball player who stands six feet nine inches tall and takes care of Brian for much of the time, helping him in his efforts to lose weight and get into better physical trim. A sister of the Love family, Maureen Love West, played harp on Mike Love's *Everyone's In Love With You* on *15 Big Ones*. As already mentioned, Carl's brother-in-law, Billy Hinsche, is a regular member of the Beach Boys when they're playing live, as well as helping out on the records. Other concert helpers include Ed Carter on guitar and Ron Altbach

on keyboards, while there's often a floating population of other connected people like the Captain and Tennille and Charles Lloyd.

Every consideration of the Beach Boys must eventually come back to Brian. After *15 Big Ones,* Brian apparently decided to manage without Eugene Landy. In many ways, that was a predictable move — whatever Brian has become involved in through his life seems to have been for short periods. Without much doubt, Landy did help Brian to pull himself together, and at least to begin creating beautiful music again. Without Landy, Brian's vision of himself as "a useless little vegetable" could have continued and worsened.

He told *Rolling Stone* that without Landy "I'd have been a goner. I'd have been in the hospital by now." It was also probably Landy who encouraged Brian to talk to the press around the time of *15 Big Ones,* something which had been rare, if not unheard of, in the several years previously. As a result, major articles appeared in *Rolling Stone, People* and *Crawdaddy* magazines, and while they didn't always portray Brian in the most flattering light, they no doubt helped him to see himself more clearly in the eyes of the outside world, and perhaps to adjust his behavior pattern accordingly. *Pet Sounds* magazine, a fanzine devoted to Beach Boys ephemera, asked Brian in yet another interview if this public dissection was hurtful. Brian felt that in some ways, it was, "It depends. Now, if they put a negative slant to me . . . I don't mind being criticized logically, take a person and logically analyze the guy and lay it out for the public. But if they knock you down, then it hurts a little bit, but I take it in my stride. I figure that you've gotta see both sides to a person. It's good for everybody to see a person as he is, to kind of check into the person, check his values out, see where he's at. It hurts a little to get knocked. Everybody gets knocked, Frank Sinatra's the same way. When he gets knocked, it hurts him. We all have our feelings. But I think, by and large, just getting written about is the main thing. I think the publicity of it all, and the feeling that you're in the limelight, that there's something to read about, this all means a lot to me."

There certainly was a glut of Brian Wilson coverage in the press, and this extended into other media too. In 1976, he even appeared on national television in America without the rest of the group. On September 18 of that year, a very smart Brian — wearing a tuxedo and slimmed down to around 210lbs (about 15 stone which is not unreasonable considering his height of 6' 3") — was nominated to the 'Rock Hall Of Fame' along with the Beatles, Bob Dylan and Elvis Presley. He accepted the honor and also announ-

Brian back where he belongs.

ced the winners of a couple of other awards. Brian told *Pet Sounds,* "The standing ovation was one of the highlights of my life, without a doubt. I almost cried. I didn't expect it. Who in the world would think they're all gonna stand up for you? I didn't expect it. I figured my peers are out there, but I didn't figure there's that many peers, that they would stand up, sort of a chain reaction, one person stands up and another person does and everything."

That wasn't the only chance American TV audiences had to see Brian, because an excellent hour-long TV special was made, also in 1976, in which he took a considerable part. The highlight of the show for many people was a part where Brian was "arrested for failure to surf," and forced to finally

indulge in the sport which he had brought alive musically. The *Rolling Stone* report described the scene. "Soberly, Brian plods forward, accompanied by Danny Aykroyd and John Belushi [of NBC's *Saturday Night*] in highway patrol uniforms. About 50 yards from the ocean they stop, and Aykroyd steps out to direct the breakers. Then he nods to Brian, and says 'OK, Mr Wilson, here's your wave.' A small crowd of friends and crew people watches nervously, silently, as Brian carries out his sentence. His feet touch the surf but he plunges ahead, up to his waist, then dives in, his whalelike body atop the board and totally immersed in the cool clear water. The crowd cheers like crazy."

Such an event would never have happened before 1976, and as if to confirm Brian's renaissance, the start of 1977 saw another new Beach Boys

WEA

album, *The Beach Boys Love You,* consisting entirely of original material — the vast majority written by Brian, and the whole album produced by him. An insert in the album sleeve bears of large picture of a smiling Brian with Marilyn, with the legend: "To Brian whom we all love with all our hearts. We wish to express our appreciation, and acknowledge your willingness to create and support totally the completion of these songs. We thank you for sharing yourself and your music with us, and all those who love you as well. An unspeakable joy being with you in your expression of the music you put out there for everyone. Brian, we feel honored and grateful and we love you. Carl, Dennis, Michael and Alan."

That affecting tribute would mean little or nothing were it not for the fact that the album in the author's estimation and that of several critics, is the best released by the group since the '60s. Nearly all the songs are new, the only exception being *Good Time,* which was previously found on the *Spring* album. There's another connection with that album in the duet between Brian and Marilyn Wilson on *Let's Put Our Hearts Together.*

Brian, interviewed for *Sounds,* also liked the album. "This is really the first time since *Pet Sounds* that I've felt this thoroughly satisfied with an album. I think it gives a little bit, it has a little extra. There's more to it than throwing the stuff in there and getting it over with and getting it out to make money. These last sessions were much more productive [than for *15 Big Ones*]. The guys were a lot happier, they seemed really with it. Of course, Mike and Al being meditators, they're always with it. Carl was a little more receptive to everything, and Dennis of course. The Beach Boys were much more receptive this time around, and I was in a much better frame of mind than I'd been in a long time, so we were able to work on the album *together.*"

The Beach Boys were, triumphantly, together again. They had survived some of the most extraordinary setbacks. What other group could have experienced such profound depths and yet still retained not only their identity but also — and more amazing — the respect and affection of the public? The Beach Boys have fluctuated between enormous acclaim and extreme (if sometimes deserved) criticism. As Dennis Wilson said, "I can tell you the day the Beach Boys will no longer exist — never. We'll be on stage in wheelchairs." And doubtless there will be a large number of similarly mobile people in the audience to watch!

US Discography

This is intended as a guide to major releases only and does not attempt to include the many and confusing repackages. Titles, dates and companies may vary in other countries.

SINGLES

1962	Surfin'/Luau	Candix
	Surfin' Safari/409	Capitol
	Ten Little Indians/County Fair	Capitol
1963	Surfin' USA/Shut Down	Capitol
	Surfer Girl/Little Deuce Coupe	Capitol
	Be True To Your School/ In My Room	Capitol
	Little Saint Nick/The Lord's Prayer	Capitol
1964	Fun, Fun, Fun/Why Do Fools Fall In Love	Capitol
	I Get Around/Don't Worry Baby	Capitol
	When I Grow Up (To Be A Man)/She Knows Me Too Well	Capitol
	Dance, Dance, Dance/The Warmth Of The Sun	Capitol
	The Man With All The Toys/ Blue Christmas	Capitol
1965	Do You Wanna Dance?/ Please Let Me Wonder	Capitol
	Help Me, Rhonda/Kiss Me Baby	Capitol
	California Girls/Let Him Run Wild	Capitol
	The Little Girl I Once Knew/ There's No Other (Like My Baby)	Capitol
1966	Barbara-Ann/Girl Don't Tell Me	Capitol
	Sloop John B/You're So Good To Me	Capitol
	Caroline No/Summer Means New Love (Brian Wilson only)	Capitol
	God Only Knows/Wouldn't It Be Nice	Capitol
	Good Vibrations/Let's Go Away for A While	Capitol
1967	Heroes And Villains/You're Welcome	Brother/ Capitol
	Gettin' Hungry/Devoted To You (Brian Wilson & Mike Love)	Brother
	Wild Honey/Wind Chimes	Capitol
	Darlin'/Here Today	Capitol
1968	Friends/Little Bird	Capitol
	Do It Again/Wake The World	Capitol
	Bluebirds Over The Mountain/ Never Learn Not To Love	Capitol
1969	I Can Hear Music/All I Want To Do	Capitol
	Break Away/Celebrate The News	Capitol
1970	Cottonfields/The Nearest Faraway Place	Capitol
	Slip On Through/This Whole World	Brother/ Reprise
	Tears In The Morning/It's About Time	Brother/ Reprise
	Cool, Cool Water/Forever	Brother/ Reprise
1971	Long Promised Road/'Til I Die	Brother/ Reprise
	Wouldn't It Be Nice/	Ode
	Long Promised Road/'Til I Die (re-release)	Brother/ Reprise
	Surf's Up/Don't Go Near The Water	Brother/ Reprise
1972	You Need A Mess of Help To Stand Alone/Cuddle Up	Brother/ Reprise
	Marcella/Hold On Dear Brother	Brother/ Reprise
1973	Sail On Sailor/The Trader	Brother/ Reprise
	California Saga (On My Way Sunny Californ-I-Ay)/Funky Pretty	Brother/ Reprise
1974	Surfin' USA/ (reissue)	Capitol
	Child Of Winter/Susie Cincinnati	Brother/ Reprise
1975	Sail On Sailor/Only With You	Brother/ Reprise
1976	Rock And Roll Music/ TM Song	Brother/ Reprise
	It's OK/Had To Phone Ya	Brother/ Reprise

Capitol

ALBUMS

1962	Surfin' Safari	Capitol
1963	Surfin' USA	Capitol
	Shut Down – Volume 1 *(BB's plus others)*	Capitol
	Surfer Girl	Capitol
	Little Deuce Coupe	Capitol
1964	Shut Down – Volume 2	Capitol
	All Summer Long	Capitol
	The Beach Boys' Christmas Album	Capitol
	The Beach Boys' Concert	Capitol
1965	The Beach Boys Today	Capitol
	Summer Days (And Summer Nights!)	Capitol
	The Beach Boys' Party	Capitol
1966	Pet Sounds	Capitol
	Best Of The Beach Boys – Volume 1	Capitol
1967	Smiley Smile	Brother
	Best Of The Beach Boys – Volume 2	Capitol
	Deluxe Set: Pet Sounds/ Summer Days (And Summer Nights!)/Today	Capitol
	Wild Honey	Capitol
1968	Friends	Capitol
	Best Of The Beach Boys – Volume 3	Capitol
	Stack O'Tracks	Capitol
1969	20/20	Capitol
	Greatest Hits	Capitol
1970	Sunflower	Brother/ Reprise
1971	Surf's Up	Brother/ Reprise
1972	Carl & The Passions – So Tough/Pet Sounds	Brother/ Reprise
1973	Holland	Brother/ Reprise
	The Beach Boys In Concert	Brother/ Reprise
1974	Endless Summer	Capitol
	Wild Honey & 20/20	Brother/ Reprise
	Friends & Smiley Smile	Brother/ Reprise
1975	Spirit of America	Capitol
	Good Vibrations (Best Of)	Brother/ Reprise
1976	15 Big Ones	Brother/ Reprise
1977	Live In London	Capitol
	The Beach Boys Love You	Brother/ Reprise